INTERNET BASED LEARNING

INTERNET BASED LEARNING

An Introduction and Framework for
Higher Education and Business

EDITED BY *Deanie French, Charles Hale,
Charles Johnson,* and *Gerald Farr*

KOGAN
PAGE

LONDON

First published in 1999

Apart from any fair dealing for the purposes of research or private study,
or criticism or review, as permitted under the Copyright, Designs and
Patents Act 1988, this publication may only be reproduced, stored or
transmitted, in any form or by any means, with the prior permission in
writing of the publishers, or in the case of reprographic reproduction in
accordance with the terms and licences issued by the CLA. Enquiries
concerning reproduction outside these terms should be sent to the
publishers at the undermentioned address:

Published out side U.S.A. and Canada by
KOGAN PAGE LIMITED
120 Pentonville Road
London N1 9JN

Published in U.S.A and Canada by **STYLUS PUBLISHING, LLC**

© STYLUS PUBLISHING LLC, 1999

British Library Cataloguing in Publication Data
A CIP record for this book is available from the British Library.

ISBN 0 7494 2935 6 Paperback
ISBN 0 7494 2936 4 Hardback

Typeset, printed and bound in the USA
Printed on acid free paper

To all educators and trainers
joining the adventure of enhancing learning with the Internet

Contents

Acknowledgments

First, I would like to thank our editor John von Knorring for finding my first article about Cyber-learning on the Internet and then contacting me by email to develop the book. This book would not have been possible without his partnership. He supplied an endless stream of questions and ideas to continually raise the quality of this project. I thank him for his guidance and patience.

Thanks to the experts with Southwest Texas University who work with faculty to assist them in obtaining Internet-based skills. Mike Ferris, director of Media Services, taught me several years ago the difference between producing an electronic handout versus interactive lessons. He and his staff provided excellent support for collaboration and resources for development and testing of a homepage, listserv, chat room, and many other Internet-based innovations.

Thanks to Gerald Farr, director of the Faculty Advancement Center, for organizing faculty development workshops and a special summer workshop "Excellence in Teaching," which taught faculty how to use multimedia on the Internet.

Thanks to James Andrews, director of Correspondence and Extension, and his staff for their encouragement and support for the development of Southwest Texas University's first virtual course for academic credit.

Thanks to Rumaldo Jurez, dean of the School of Health Professions at Southwest Texas University, for his support of technology-based learning options and his endorsement of innovations in teaching.

Thanks to Dr. Charles Johnson, chair of the Department of Health Services and

Research at Southwest Texas University for his continued visionary leadership and personal participation in Internet innovation.

Thanks to Frank Fuller and Bob Gillan for their assistance to Steve Bett in the early development stages of the manuscript development.

Thanks to the many students who have helped me learn more effective ways to utilize the Internet. Collaboration with students in the utilization of Internet-based innovation has enriched my professional life and added spark to my teaching.

Thanks to all the individuals who gave permission for their picture to be included: Leslie Bidwell, Charles Hale, Lori Hooks, Daniel Ludwig Bob Mooney Kelly Reyna, Kathi Ritch, Dawn Rusing, and Yvonne Voltz.

Thanks to all those individuals who allowed us to use screen dumps from their Web sites: Randy Bass (Georgetown University), Rev. Raymond Bucko (Le Moyne College), Steven Buehler (S &B Computers), Lisa Gye (Swinburne University), Joan Fleitas, (Fairfield University), Lynn Holt (Mississippi State University), Matej Lexa (University of Illinois), Paul Miesing (University of Albany), Doug Marchio (University of Maine), Marsha Morgan (University of Texas), Jim Segers (Texas A&M University), David Sharpe (University of Ohio), Bruce Spear (Humboldt University Berlin), John Seydel (Arkansas State University), and John Stephens (American Studies Association).

A very special thank you to Dr. John Durrett for his insightful critique and suggestions for improvements to the manuscript.

I would like to thank my daughter Anna and her husband for providing a Mexico City "get a-way" for developing the book proposal; and to my other daughter Wendy for her frequent beside-the-computer chats while I was working.

Last, I would like to thank Arlene for her assistance in the creative process.

Introduction

INTERNET-BASED LEARNING: A FRAMEWORK AND INTRODUCTION

FOR HIGHER EDUCATION AND BUSINESS

Technological answers are being provided before most of us fully understand the questions. This is truly an enchanted time of change in education. This book is designed for junior college faculty, senior college faculty, and business trainers who wish to integrate new Internet technology for learning. The move to integrate the Internet in teaching and learning is rapidly gaining momentum. Learning options over the Internet are increasingly expanding and are becoming part of the routine landscape of education and training.

This book is for every educator and trainer who wants to use the Internet's instructional opportunities even if his or her own personal computer skills are limited.

The framework for this book is based on the following assumptions.

Augmented Teaching

Augmented teaching is based on the assumption that educators can enrich current teaching styles by augmenting classes with aspects of Internet-based learning. The augmenting teaching style incorporates current styles, while at the same time suggesting that courses be enhanced with the addition of one or more Internet-based activities. Augmented classes use everything from e-mail to slide shows on the Internet to multiple, interconnected electronic formats.

Virtual Learning

The educational process of learning over the Internet without having face-to-face contact is known as *virtual learning*. Learning can be individualized through virtual classes. Learners use self-directed learning principles to master content at their own rate, at times convenient to the learner, either from work or home. The Internet replaces conventional lecture halls and classrooms, creating new opportunities and challenges for teachers and learners.

Progressive Application

The ongoing process of applying Internet-based technology to education while skills and confidence develop is known as *progressive application*. Learning can occur within work hours to take advantage of the facilities and expertise available on campus or at the office. "Just-in-time learning," which is the process of having educational access available at the time the learner wishes to start learning at home or at work applies to the educator as well as the student. As the teacher, you are encouraged to match your level of Internet skills with the variety of learning options available. There is no need to suddenly learn HTML programming for the Web. You can begin as simply as using e-mail discussions between you and others, and then progress to more advanced Internet applications as your experience grows. The important step is the one you take now—deciding that you want to expand your knowledge of Internet-based Learning (IBL) to continue your personal education and want to use your knowledge of Internet-based teaching to improve your teaching options. The ever-expanding technology and information of the Internet offer amazing opportunities to integrate and enhance the current way you teach.

A caution, though, one can jump in over one's head—we suggest that you begin by wading in the shallows.

Objectives

At the end of this book, readers will be able to:

1. Identify business and educational uses of Internet-based learning.

2. Specify skills needed for self-directed learning.

3. Identify the importance of learning to learn.

4. Apply the model of situated learning for adults.

5. Increase overall awareness of Internet-based teaching options to augment classes.

6. Identify models of Internet-based teaching in different fields of study.

7. Progress from using the internet to augment courses, to creating virtual courses.

8. Use virtual learning for individualized instruction.

9. Utilize progressive steps to build Internet-based learning.

10. Utilize evaluation measures for Internet activities.

11. Identify elements needed for creating a complete on-line learning environment.

12. Ponder perspectives for the future.

13. Feel inspired to apply concepts from the book.

14. Utilize a related ongoing Internet web site. Available on-line at:
     http://www.swt.edu/~df12/Internet/right.htm

Chapter Overviews

CHAPTER 1: PREPARING FOR INTERNET-BASED LEARNING

DEANIE FRENCH

This chapter provides the foundation skills needed to transition from total teacher control of learning activities to incorporation of self-directed opportunities. We have now reached a point in time when both the teacher *and* learner need to become continual learners to adapt to rapidly changing information. Many students and faculty find this shift of role and thinking an exciting development that provides new challenges for assimilation and application of new concepts. Other teachers have not yet accepted the Internet as a source of quality information or as a course delivery system. When educators give lectures, they know the quality of the information that is presented. In contrast, sharing teaching roles with the Internet can be intimating. Also, many teachers and students find it difficult to switch to new roles and ways of processing information. *Cognitive restructuring*, changing the way learners think, is presented as a method to assist in developing self-directed learning. Twelve basic skills are identified as a way to help students change the way they think about self-directed learning.

CHAPTER 2: LEARNING TO LEARN IN A WWW-BASED ENVIRONMENT
BETTY COLLIS AND ENRICO MEEUWSEN

When students use the WWW for a learning environment, they can have the world at their fingertips. At the click of a search engine, such as Yahoo and Lycos, people and resources from all over the world can be at the students' computers. The learning opportunities are enormous! But, does it work out this way in practice? How does the student respond to all of this potential?

Collis and Meeuwsen have observed important differences among students as they make use of the WWW as a learning environment. Some students quickly find and build upon new ideas; others look at the screen and wonder what to do. This led the authors to think carefully about the sorts of skills and approaches to learning students need in order to make creative and constructive use of the learning potential of the WWW. In particular, they believe skills related to "learning how to learn" are of key importance. The authors describe some of these learning-to-learn skills that are most helpful for students, demonstrating from their teaching how they are trying to help the students develop these skills at the same time as they participate in a WWW-based course.

CHAPTER 3: AUGMENTING TRADITIONAL TEACHING WITH INTERNET-BASED OPTIONS
STEVE BETT, DEANIE FRENCH, GERALD FARR, AND LORI HOOKS

This chapter builds on the information presented in chapters 1 and 2 by providing examples of the Internet to augment current course delivery in a variety of disciplines. This chapter provides examples of Internet-based learning practices of several college-level teachers who are at all levels of sophistication and experience. For those contemplating a transition to Internet-based learning the important concept to remember is that each of the teachers discussed in this section were once beginners. They made a decision to investigate the utility of Internet-based activities in their classes, and to start down a path of continuing growth and development. It is a never-ending path. You can travel down this path as quickly as you desire, stopping or slowing when you feel uncomfortable, and adopting what you believe will work best for your classes and students. It's important, however, that you begin the trip.

CHAPTER 4: SKILLS FOR DEVELOPING, UTILIZING AND EVALUATING INTERNET-BASED LEARNING

DEANIE FRENCH

This chapter presents progressively sophisticated ways to integrate Web-based technology into education or training settings. Six skill areas are described to help you become more technology enabled for IBL: (1) Building electronic interpersonal relations through e-networking, (2) Harvesting the Internet for information, (3) Assessing Websites for quality, appearance, and technical performance; (4) Developing self-directed modules, (5) Creating an effective online course manager to blend course elements, and (6) Using of collaborative learning.

CHAPTER 5: INTERNET-BASED LEARNING TOOLS— EXAMPLES OF USE FROM INDUSTRY

DAVE HARRIS

Harris reviews different modes of IBL such as e-mail, listservs, static Web pages, Web-based bulletin boards, chat, online courses and Electronic Performance Support Systems (EPSS) to show how they are being employed in business environments.

CHAPTER 6: INTERNET-BASED LEARNING— WHAT'S IN IT FOR THE ADULT LEARNER?

BARBARA LYMAN

This chapter introduces a useful tool for evaluating the design and delivery of education—the *Model of Situated Learning*. The model identifies the four factors that impact the effectiveness of any educational experience: (1) The characteristics of the learner; (2) The goals of the learner; (3) The nature of the learning method used, and; (4) Appropriate learning strategies. Lyman applies the model specifically to use of the Internet in adult education, and outlines how Internet-based learning can remove barriers to greater participation in education by adults. Lyman identifies a number of problems providers must address to maximize the medium's potential for this audience.

CHAPTER 7: INTERNET BASED LEARNING AND THE VIRTUAL CLASSROOM

DEANIE FRENCH, SANDY RANSOM, AND STEVE BETT

Virtual classes meet on the Internet. Students retrieve information via telephone, modem, and computer from anywhere in the world. A virtual class is not limited by geographical location, time, or space. This chapter provides examples of virtual classrooms. Most current virtual classes are offered through already established traditional university distance-education programs or business distance-learning centers. However, virtual classes are beginning to enter mainstream degree-oriented academic department offerings. The chapter ends with a description of a virtual university in Malaysia.

CHAPTER 8: CREATING A COMPLETE LEARNING ENVIRONMENT

DAVE HARRIS

This chapter focuses on the learning environment that must be developed, implemented, and supported for Internet-based learning to be successful. This chapter emphasizes that the learning environment includes not only the *content,* but also the *tools* and *infrastructure* to deliver the content. These three layers make up a complete learning experience. If any one of the three layers fails, or is too difficult to deal with, the learning experience will fail. Internet-based learning must include not only appropriately designed content, but implementation, training, and support for the infrastructure and tools' layers as well.

CHAPTER 9: WEB-RELATED ASSESSMENT AND EVALUATION

CHARLES HALE AND DEANIE FRENCH

Adding new methods for delivering instruction will not do away with one very important aspect of teaching—teachers must still be able to assess the outcome of any educational process: whether or not the intended level of learning was achieved, and if there are ways in which a course or curriculum can be improved. This chapter has four goals: (1) Provide key concepts for evaluation terms and standards; (2) Provide online assessment tools; (3) Identify components for Internet-based evaluation; and (4) Provide instruments that can be used offline or online to measure learning outcomes.

CHAPTER **10:** PERSPECTIVES ON THE FUTURE OF INTERNET-BASED LEARNING

CHARLES JOHNSON

This book concludes with an outline of likely structural changes in higher education and of technological developments in digital, multimedia, and telecommunications technologies to prepare educators and trainers for future change.

Preparing for Internet-based Learning

Deanie French

Introduction

The Internet has the potential for effecting fundamental changes in the design of learning processes, and the structures and the institutions that support it. According Marina Stock McIsaac:

> The role of the teacher of tomorrow will change. He or she will not be an actor of transmission of just consumption, but will become a facilitator of learning and research as a whole process. Therefore, teachers need to be trained in order to have new conceptions about education, strategies for learning, innovative curriculum skills, technical skills, methodology skills, a global or international perspective, and people skills to become human service educators (1995).

McIsaac points out that in reshaping education we must acquire a new conception and bravery about roles and learning. She stresses the need to build a new paradigm, a new form of thinking and of doing education. Self-directed learning is a foundation strategy for this new paradigm.

The Self-directed Learning Structure as a Foundation

To expand and enhance the role of education, educators can best take advantage of technology developments by progressively learning more about the Internet and the self-directed learning process. Effective use of the Internet as a teaching tool requires that the concept of self-directed learning be understood in order to release more control of the learning process to the student. *Self-directed learning* places the learner rather than the teacher in charge for some or most of the learning process. *Internet-based learning* is the electronic delivery of information via computer, modem, and a phone line. This form of teaching is not an all or nothing proposition. At the most basic, educators may still lecture but use the Internet to augment their presentation to make available lecture notes, slides, and syllabi. A teacher can also deliver an entire course over the Internet. For students to use Internet-based materials effectively and move away from regarding the teacher as "sage on the stage," they must learn to become self-directed and to not remain passive receptors of knowledge. The ultimate goal is to increase access to knowledge and facilitate learners becoming life-long learners.

Self-directed Learning in Business

One industry advocate sees distance and self-directed Internet-based learning as strong assets for companies. According to B. Howell, a training consultant, "employees who see themselves in a learning environment add value to companies, increase productivity, are more accepting of change, and can adapt to movement within the company" (1997). Howell continues by identifying specific benefits:

- There is no lost work time as employees can train on the job or after hours.
- The cost is lower for actual learning—the cost for travel, food, lodging, and training locations is eliminated.

- The focus is on comprehensive training—teaching employees how to learn rather than just teaching one or two skills per training course. This decreases costs and increases self-worth of employees.

- Trainers design courses which offer an individualized, self-paced approach appropriate for the adult learner; and offer students continuing attention and support via email or phone.

- Courses are customized. Case studies, examples, questions, and assistance are tailored to meet each company's specific training needs.

- Greater retention is achieved through evaluation. Evaluations are given throughout training to ensure that each employee understands and can use the new knowledge to increase job performance.

- Employees can immediately apply what they learn to their jobs because training takes place in the work environment.

- Professionals face increasing requirements for continuing education hours. Internet-based learning will meet the needs of professionals who find it hard to leave work to attend conferences.

Self-directed Learning in Higher Education

Some educators are skeptical that self-directed learning can be effective for teaching academic content, which has been traditionally been taught through lectures. Typically, credit for courses has been limited to those taught on campus or those delivered through the

correspondence office. Whether a course is taught by a faculty member as part of an in-load or out-of-load assignment through the correspondence office, the student still earns the same three hours of academic credit. However, in the U.S. federal scholarship regulations only recognize traditionally taught courses and do not allow students to count correspondence courses for financial assistance under the general mandate that students must be enrolled for at least nine hours of academic courses to be fulltime students. This rule reinforces traditional beliefs and attitudes about the value of class attendance as a necessary condition for significant learning.

The Internet threatens to make some types of campus-dependent learning obsolete. Educators need to consider how technology will affect the entire process of teaching and learning. This doesn't mean that teachers have to accept an all or nothing approach toward self-directed learning or Internet-based learning. However, educators, who have themselves learned through lectures and have been successful in using lecture methodology, may want to consider gradually integrating Internet-based learning. There are several ways educators can expand lectures by augmenting their current style of teaching, such as putting new versions of handouts on the Internet to cut down on printing costs, or by making course assignments available on the World Wide Web.

Development of the Concept of Self-directed Learning

I began researching self-directed learning as the focus of my doctoral dissertation in the early 1970s. At that time *self-directed learning* was contrasted with *teacher-directed learning*. My professors predicted that self-directed learning would be a reality in the '80s. It is now almost the year 2000 and most education and training still relies on lectures.

A few students and teachers find the shift from teacher-directed to self-directed learning to be an exciting option. However, the majority of students and teachers find it difficult to switch to new roles and new ways of processing information. Students tend to be reluctant to adopt new styles of learning. But, if learning combines both lecture and student-directed learning, students will gain an additional learning tool. In other words, students will benefit from having a teacher who is a sage part of the time and an Internet guide at other times. It makes sense to offer students both forms of learning.

Restructured Education

The term *restructuring education* describes a shift in educational focus. In 1992, there were over 2,500 ERIC entries for the term *restructured education*. It has become commonplace to contrast depictions of the teacher as "sage on the stage" versus a "guide on the side." Now we have reached a point in time where both the teacher and learner are simultaneously "guides" and "sages," as all of us become continual learners and peer teachers adapting rapidly to changing information.

In March 1992, I attended and presented two papers at the Ninth International Conference on Technology and Education in Paris. A major theme of this conference was restructuring education through technology. Most of the presentations focused on elementary schools and secondary education. However, it is only now that higher education is catching up with elementary and secondary sectors.

Ann Ward, of the National School Board Association's Institute for the Transfer of Technology to Education, further clarified *restructuring* as "calling for a new mode of education," that:

- Is personalized for each pupil.

- Is cross-curricular.

- Involves active learning.

- Features cooperative learning groups.

- Empowers students to take responsibility for their own learning.

- Empowers the teacher to be a learning coach rather than a "sage on stage."

Ward summarized what was rapidly evolving in our public schools systems as early as 1992. Five years later, industry is leading higher education in the move away from traditional teaching and training roles to encouraging learners to take charge of their learning.

Instructivist Versus Constructivist

Another way to view differences in student learning is to compare the instructivist and constructivist approaches. There is a considerable amount of information in the literature about this subject. Brooks and Brooks (1995) present a useful comparison of instructivist and constructivist approaches. Five of their concepts are highlighted in Table 1.1.

TABLE 1.1. COMPARISON OF INSTRUCTIVIST AND CONSTRUCTIVIST APPROACHES

INSTRUCTIVIST	CONSTRUCTIVIST
1. Teacher writes the objectives.	1. Objectives are written with student collaboration based on the learner's needs.
2. Objectives are written for all in hierarchical form and sequenced from simple to complex.	2. Stresses the importance of divergence based on the uniqueness of the learner.
3. Learners are seen as passive or as holes to be filled with static data.	3. Problems are solved that have personal relevance to learners.
4. Knowledge is separate from knowing.	4. Knowledge is individual and socially constructed, based on personal experiences.
5. Learning consists of acquiring "truth" or the ability to mimic and can be measured with tests.	5. Learning can only be measured through direct observation and dialogue.

In their book *The Case for Constructivist Classroom* (1995), Brooks and Brooks offer twelve practical strategies for developing constructivist teaching:

1. Constructivist teachers encourage and accept student autonomy and initiative.

2. Constructivist teachers use raw data and primary sources, along with manipulative, interactive, and physical materials.

3. When framing tasks, constructivist teachers use cognitive terminology such as "classify," "analyze," "predict," and "create."

4. Constructivist teachers allow student responses to drive lessons, shift instructional strategies, and alter content.

5. Constructivist teachers inquire about students' understanding of concepts before sharing their own understandings of those concepts.

6. Constructivist teachers encourage students to engage in dialogue, both with the teacher and with one another.

7. Constructivist teachers encourage student inquiry by asking thoughtful, open-ended questions and encouraging students to ask questions of each other.

8. Constructivist teachers seek elaboration of students' initial responses.

9. Constructivist teachers engage students in experiences that might engender contradictions

to their initial hypotheses and then encourage discussion.

10. Constructivist teachers allow waiting time after posing questions.

11. Constructivist teachers provide time for students to construct relationships and create metaphors.

12. Constructivist teachers nurture students' natural curiosity through frequent use of the learning cycle model. (The learning cycle model consists of discovery, concept introduction, and concept application. [Chiu 1995].)

For greater understanding, you may wish to proceed on a self-directed basis and find a peer to discuss the following.

1. How would these strategies work in your setting?

2. Do the terms have practical meaning for you?

3. Will they have greater influence in the near future?

Instructivist "teacher-directed learning" and constructivist "student-directed learning" represent two poles in a a continuum of teacher and student behaviors. Neither is better than the other. Educators will pick and choose as their philosophy and circumstance dictates.

Comparing Control of Learning Variables

In self-directed learning who controls the variables? Before the Web, teachers tended to control and organize all the activities and resources and then lead the students to them in a sequential fashion. However, with the Internet, control is increasingly being relinquished to the learner, potentially enhancing the entire learning experience. Now students can find an amazing, enriching, and divergent set of articles and resources, of which the educator may not be aware.

Some years ago, I realized the need to provide a foundation before having the learner embark on self-directed learning quest with modules. Students (and teachers) need to change the way they think about the teaching/learning process. What are the behaviors needed in self-directed learning? The operational definition in the next section is an ongoing developmental process. Its purpose is to identify the most useful and effective behaviors for self-directed learning.

Definition of Self-directed Learning (1977 to present)

In 1977, the American Nurses' Association Ad Hoc Committee on Nontraditional Learning developed a definition of self-directed learning. The committee—of which I was a member—struggled to identify components of self-directed learning that would facilitate the acceptance of a variety of self-directed approaches to learning for nurses in an industry that requires Continuing Education Units (CEUs) for licensure. This committee defined *self-directed learning* as "an activity for which the learner takes the initiative and responsibility for the learning process."

Depending on the design of this activity, the learner may have a choice or control over one or more of the following learning variables:

- assessment of learning needs
- objectives or learning outcomes
- environment
- time
- pace
- appropriate sequence
- appropriate experiences
- human and nonhuman resources
- method(s) of evaluation and
- method(s) of documenting that objectives are met

The committee then broadened the concept by noting that that these variables can be incorporated into a *self-designed* learning experience or a *teacher-designed* learning experience. This chapter will present primarily a teacher-designed format for self-directed learning.

Operational Definition for Cognitive Restructuring: Changing the Way Students Think

Most students in my undergraduate courses still want to be taught as they have always been taught. I have found that teaching the operational definitions of self-directed

FIGURE 1.1 OPERATIONAL DEFINITIONS OF TWELVE SELF-DIRECTED LEARNING SKILLS

1. **Analyzing Learning Options**
   Identifying, evaluating, and exploring a wide range of resources to learn the same content.

2. **Information Ignorance**
   Accepting that the proliferation of information has made it impossible to review and analyze all the sources of information about a specific topic.

3. **Choosing Alternatives**
   Recognizing the value of testing and adapting resources to meet personal learning needs.

4. **Helping Peers Learn**
   Learning to value teaching others as an effective way to learn and reinforce basic knowledge.

5. **Handling Rapid Change**
   Continually identifying and prioritizing areas in which to update skills.

6. **Tolerating Ambiguity**
   Comfortably exploring alternative interpretations and handling uncertainty.

7. **Resilience to Failure**
   Recognizing that temporary setbacks are part of mastering new skills, particularly high technology skills.

8. **Self-Reward**
   Recognizing the intrinsic value of learning rather than being motivated by external rewards from teachers.

9. **Openness to a New Style of Learning**
   Understanding the value of alternative methods of learning

10. **Integrating Technology**
    Overcoming barriers to use of technology and incorporating new technology as part of the learning process.

11. **Asking Teachers for Help**
    Seeking help from teachers or other experts.

12. **Asking Peers for Help**
    Accepting that collaborative learning depends on mutual assistance.

learning at the very beginning of a course helps students to transition to self-directed behaviors. For the past several years, I have been attempting to use cognitive restructuring for learning as a process for introducing self-directed modules. I have taught twelve basic skills designed to change the way students think about learning (see figure 1.1).

In the spring 1997, I asked fifty undergraduates who were enrolled in an introductory computer course to use their own terms to describe these skills. Their answers were incorporated into the above operational definitions. A *basic definition* is a statement about the meaning of a term. (Webster 1991). In contrast, an *operational definition* is derived from the process being used. (Webster 1991). The behaviors identified work together to achieve successful self-directed learning experiences. Developing and refining the skills is an ongoing process. The need and importance of each of the twelve skills varies from individual to individual.

Not all of these behaviors are absolutely necessary to achieve self-directed learning skills. What's important is a desire to change. However, the more these behaviors are mastered, the more likely a student will become successful in this mode of learning. Some students have more difficulty than others.

I have collected qualitative and quantitative data over several years which indicates that students can change their manner of learning. An ongoing qualitative analysis with graduate and undergraduate focus groups revealed that difficulties related to mastering new patterns of learning revolve around barriers for four of the self-directed learning skills. In the fall of 1991, a t-test was employed to test paired differences among a group of seventeen upper-level undergraduates enrolled in a training class to compare their pre- and post-test attitudes about self-directed-learning. The post-test scores indicated a significantly greater willingness by students to be directly responsible for the learning process. These results indicate that while most students enter university classes primarily with linear-based learning strategies, they can master new behaviors to facilitate restructured learning. It is assumed that this is true for business settings.

Potential Barrier #1: Self-reward Versus Teacher's Reward

Many students have difficulty identifying and accepting intrinsic rewards instead of external rewards from faculty or other authority figures. Only a few learn just for the joy of learning.

Among the advantages of Internet-based learning are the hypertext links that let students go seamlessly from one link to another. Finding updated and new information is intrinsically exciting. Serendipitous learning is a great way to expand basic knowledge. As students learn to explore new areas of related ideas, their knowledge base expands.

Unfortunately, many students use the standard of "what's on the test" to determine what is most important to learn. Concern about the test cuts the excitement of exploration

short, setting up a conflict between choosing "what do I want to learn" with "what do I think the teacher will expect me to know." The students receiving a good grade on a "churn and learn" basis reinforce the value of test-driven knowledge acquisition.

While the Internet offers enormous learning resources, many educators may have trouble accepting the value of this type of divergent learning and even more difficulty in determining a grade for information that the student learns which is not officially sanctioned by the educator. Yet, never before has there been so much information available with many enticing trails for students to follow. Concerns can be decreased as educators and students learn guidelines for assessing the quality of Internet-based information (see chapter 9, "Web Related Assessment and Evaluation").

The goal of self-directed learning is to help students learn the process in order that they can become self-directed and reward themselves for having obtained the knowledge. Throughout their lives they will be continual learners and will need these skills.

Potential Barrier # 2: Adding New Styles of Learning

On completion of their course, most of my students have indicated that they enjoyed self-directed learning and looked forward to other courses that use this style of teaching. However, a number of students, particularly undergraduates, felt a teacher is needed to help them identify all important information.

Students who cling to learning only by lecture will miss many future educational opportunities for personal development and professional continuing education. Limiting one's options narrows one's opportunities.

Potential Barrier # 3: Asking Peers for Help

Former educational programming equates asking for help with cheating. Until the climate is changed and learners accept the fact that they need help, they will probably learn more slowly and experience unnecessary frustration.

Potential Barrier # 4: Changing Role of the Teacher

Both teacher and students have to grapple with the idea of the teacher not having to be in front of the classroom, or even inside the classroom, to dispense knowledge. My methodology is to structure class work around modules. While developing modules is time intensive, once developed they are relatively easy to revise and to continually improve.

Almost every course, if not all the courses I teach, have self-directed learning modules that are developed before the course begins. Once I have finished a class, I can revise and improve my modules each semester based on feedback from learners. It is not unusual to have problems with a module the first time it is presented. I find students are more than willing to tell me how to improve the components.

More information about designing and building modules can be found in chapter 4, "Skills for Developing, Utilizing and Evaluating Internet-based Learning." Figure 1.2 identifies the critical components of a module. There is also a sample module found in Appendix 7.1.

Modules allow the teacher to assume a greater role as guide because time that would

FIGURE 1.2 MODULE COMPONENTS FOR SELF-DIRECTED LEARNING

1. Descriptive title with module number.

2. Lists of module objectives with the traditional clause: When you have successfully completed this module you will (or should) be able to:

3. Overview of the module and an introduction to the content to be learned.

4. Reading assignments from textbook, articles, etc. If there is no reading assignment, write "none."

5. Web assignments. If the module is online, the Web assignments can be hyper-linked. If the module is handed out to students, the URL or address of the Web site needs to be given. If there is no Web assignment, write "none."

6. Finishing the assignment—what is needed and when. List all of the products or assignments the student needs to complete and when they are due.

7. Practice test (optional). An online practice test is effective when delivering information in an online course.

8. Evaluation form for the module. This form can be online or offline.

9. Encouragement of questions through email.

10. Link to other online modules.

---

otherwise be spent lecturing can be used to facilitate small group work, to promote peer interaction, and to answer individual questions.

PALS: A System to Help Overcome Barriers to Self-directed Learning.

Learning through technology can be a challenge for many adults. *Peer–assisted learning* (PALS) facilitates the educational process of utilizing technology for enhanced learning. There are many different types of peer-assisted learning. Since peer-assisted learning has achieved greater popularity at lower grade levels, students with experience of it will eventually be entering higher education and the workforce. They will expect more options than traditional-based education.

Vanderbilt Partnerships for Education (1996) describes PALS as a process where the teachers reshape the learning environment so that every student in the class is paired with another student for a portion of the school day. Each pair then works on structured activities in reading and math designed to meet the pair's individual needs. In this way, teachers can differentiate the instruction to address individual students' learning needs. Students are trained in methods for interacting in a tutoring session. Each PALS session is reciprocal, allowing both students to participate as tutor and student. PALS was developed for students in first through sixth grades. This system has been evaluated by the U.S. Department of Education's Program Effectiveness Panel and has been recognized as an effective instructional method.

Peer-Assisted Learning: Blending Teacher-directed Learning and Self-directed Learning

My ongoing qualitative research with focus groups each semester continues to shape use of PALS. In some situations, I match students and at other times I allow self-selection. If students already know each other, then self-selection may be the preferred choice. As in life, not all pairing makes for greater understanding of the content and deepened problem solving. I allow students to change partners any time there is an apparent conflict. For guidelines, see Figure 1.3.

I encourage teamwork when possible and challenge the students to learn new ways of interacting with each other. When I use Internet-based collaborative learning, I assign members of two pairs to the same team. Recently, many students commented that they found this assignment created new skills for interacting with "distant" members. One student this semester was amazed at his ability to work with an "invisible" person. Some students did not like the required extra work required to interact with people who were not sitting next to them, but also expressed surprise at the quality of the outcomes. Learning to build electronic interpersonal relations will become increasingly important each year as our society depends more on electronic communication and global collaboration.

My students also communicate between classes through electronic mail with other students and with me. Students who do not utilize e-mail substitute the telephone and fax machine for frequent exchanges of information. They are encouraged to share information and resources when completing individual self-directed learning modules. Of course, all students are held accountable for individually demonstrating understanding of key information for normative referenced testing purposes. More information about the

FIGURE 1.3: GUIDELINES FOR PEER-ASSISTED LEARNING

1. Each situation needs to be assessed to determine if peer-assisted learning enhances the learning process. In many situations, such as testing, individual assessment is generally indicated.

2. Make sure that the goal(s) of all peer-assisted learning is clear.

3. Include higher-order thinking goals such as problem solving and creativity.

4. Let the learners know that helping and sharing is encouraged and they are not cheating when they assist others in the learning process.

5. Include safeguards to ensure full participation by all members of a pair or team.

6. Establish criteria for the final project

7. Use focus groups with target groups to determine ways to fine tune the process.

   - In small groups, have the group coordinator describe the contribution of each member. Then have each member describe their own contribution.

   - With pairs it is harder to ferret out different contributions made by different people. While it is apparent that a few students may take advantage of the system, the benefits outweigh total dependence on individual work.

distinction between normative referencing testing and criterion referencing will be presented in chapter 9, "Web-related Assessment and Evaluation."

Blending Teacher-directed Learning and Self-directed Learning

While there will always be a need for traditional presentation techniques, it is helpful in the transition to Internet-based learning to adopt new methods and augment current teaching styles without necessarily using technology. Presentation can take the form of a mini lecture. Class time can also be devoted to coaching. Students can complete self-directed learning modules, wih debriefing occurring in class. Debriefing the module might include:

- Learners reporting benefits of the module
- Discussion and analysis of differences in the reports
- Suggestions to improve the module

When a class is totally online and there are no opportunities for "lectures" and interaction, then email to the entire class as a group, individual email, a news bulletin board, and/or a chat room can provide opportunities for frequent interaction with learners. In the meantime, these same electronic resources can be used with traditional classroom teaching to augment content.

Bibliography

American Nurses' Association. 1978. *Self-directed Continuing Education in Nursing.* (Kansas City).

Apple, M. 1985. "Curriculum in the Year 2000." *The Education Digest*, November, 182–86.

Bett, Steve. 1994. "Envisioning a Center for Learning Technologies." Unpublished paper. School of Education, University of Louisville.

Brookfield, S. 1993. "Self-directed Learning, Political Clarity and the Critical Practice of Adult Education." *Adult Education Quarterly*, 43, (4), 225–30.

Chittenden, E. 1991. "Authentic Assessment, Evaluation and Documentation of Student Performance." In Vito Perrone, ed., *Expanding Student Assessment (ASCD)*.

Chiu, Kit Y. 1995. "Constructivist Classrooms." (http://129.7.160.115/JNST5931/Constructivist.html)

French, Deanie. 1974. "Development of a Model for Learner-directed Instruction." Unpublished doctoral dissertation. University of Texas, Austin.

French, Deanie and Durward Bell. 1983. "Harmonizing Self-directed and Teacher-directed Approaches to Learning." *Nurse Educator*, Spring, 24–30.

Gray, Pamela. 1989. "An Alternative to PSI in the Basic Course in Speech Communication: The Structural Model of Competency-Based Instruction (SMCI)."

Howell, B. 1997. Email communication on Training and Development List TRDEV-L. February 14, 1997.

Jenkins, Yolanda. 1994. "Touching the Mind: Technology and Assessment." *The Computing Teacher*, March 1994, 6–8.

Kriegel, Robert and David Brandt. 1996. *Sacred Cows Make the Best Burgers.* (New York: Warner Books).

McIsaac, Marina Stock. 1995. "Fusion of Communications and Computing Technologies: Impact on Teachers' Education." (http://seamonkey.ed.asu.edu/~mcisaac/emc5230ld95/gaby523/finrs.html)

Webster's New World Dictionary. 1991. Third edition. (New York: Prentice Hall), 363 and 949.

Serrano, Ken. 1996. "Peer Assistance and Leadership Skills (PALS) Student Training." (http://www.esc12.tenet.edu/WorkshopDesc/974223b.html).

Spear, K. 1984. "The Paideia Proposal: The Problem of Means and Ends in General Education." *The Journal of General Education*, 79–86.

Vanderbilt Partnerships in Education. 1996. "Curriculum-Based Measurement and Peer-Assisted Learning Strategies." (http://www.vanderbilt.edu/partners/pals.html).

Learning to Learn
in a WWW-based Environment
Betty Collis and Enrico Meeuwsen

When students use the World Wide Web for a learning environment, they suddenly have the world at their fingertips. People and resources from all over the world can be at a student's computer at the click of a search engine. The learning opportunities are enormous. But, does it work out this way in practice? How does the student respond to all this potential? We have observed important differences among our own students as they make use of the WWW as a learning environment. Some quickly find and build on new ideas; others look at the screen and wonder what to do. This has led us to think carefully about the sorts of skills and learning approaches that students need to make effective and constructive use of the potential of the WWW. In particular, we believe skills related to "learning to learn" are of key importance. In this chapter we will look carefully at what is involved in learning to learn, consider why it may be difficult for many students to learn how to learn in the WWW-based environment, and show how we are trying to help our own students in learning how to learn, even as they are learning how to become multimedia designers in a WWW-based first-year course at the University of Twente.

What Do We Mean by Learning to Learn?

The phrase *learning to learn* is currently very popular in the educational literature and also in the popular press. Sometimes the phrase is used as if such a target were a remarkable new discovery for educators, and instructors are chided as if they had never considered such an aim before. But the goal is not new. On the contrary, it is core to what instructors, particularly in higher education, have always seen as the larger frame to their courses and their interactions with students.

However, just because learning to learn is not new does not mean that it has been mastered by instructors or by students. For instructors in higher education, most of whom have had no formal training themselves in educational theory and learning psychology, guiding their students toward increasingly professional and mature learning-to-learn skills generally occurs in an intuitive manner. For students, the expectation may be a more painful and explicit confrontation, as those who do not meet it are frequently those who drop out or are dissatisfied. At the very least, we could hypothesize that the intellectual and professional gain that students acquire via their experiences in a higher education institution are in direct proportion to the extent they have learned how to learn from their opportunities.

MAKING THE ABSTRACT CONCRETE:
DECOMPOSING LEARNING-TO-LEARN INTO COMPONENT SKILLS

Such a strong hypothesis demands some elaboration. Learning to learn seems a self-evident phrase, but how can it be decomposed into components? If we as instructors in higher education are to be more effective in helping our students develop these components, particularly in novel teaching and learning situations such as those making use of WWW-based environments, we must be articulate about the components ourselves. Unfortunately, despite the intuitive simplicity of the idea, learning to learn has no simple nor standard definition nor any common set of guidelines for the instructor. References can be sought from a variety of sources, including educational theory and cognitive psychology. From a number of reviews of the literature (see Dunlap 1997), the following are among the core components of learning to learn:

1. Becoming aware of one's own thinking and thinking patterns. Being able to articulate what one is thinking and why one comes to conclusions. Becoming an "epistomologist." Becoming more reflective.

2. Becoming a better planner and a better self-regulator of one's own planning. Being able to adjust one's actions in order to keep on task and on tempo. Poor time management is closely related to poor planning skills.

3. Developing better study habits—a complex term involving the interaction of many content-specific skills such as better note taking and better identification of core ideas in study material—as well as developing related meta-skills, such as better self discipline, concentration, and attention to task.

4. Developing skills in finding relevant examples and models and applying them to one's own problem.

5. Developing better self-evaluation skills—the ability to anticipate areas of improvement in one's work or thinking, and look for ways to improve. (Self-evaluation is itself a meta-skill, drawing on skills in the previous four components.)

To discuss these concisely, we give each of these five components a brief label, and in the following sets of points we illustrate each with a pair of anecdotal comments to describe students with relatively weak and strong skills. We see our own students in each of these examples, whether or not WWW environments are part of the learning situation.

LEARNING-TO-LEARN COMPONENTS ILLUSTRATED

ARTICULATION AND REFLECTION

- Example of weaker development: Doesn't think about his or her thinking processes, studying means reading what is assigned.

- Example of stronger development: Reflects on why he or she has come to a certain conclusion, or why he or she feels confused. Analyses his or her own thought processes.

PLANNING SKILLS

- Example of weaker development: Does not budget time effectively at the start of a task.

Spends time dysfunctionally during a task, fails to monitor or adjust his or her time and tempo.

- Example of stronger development: Refers regularly to planning, expresses planning with charts or other schemes, adjusts the time spent on subtasks in order to achieve a good overall tempo.

STUDY SKILLS

- Example of weaker development: Loses concentration, wastes time while studying, and lacks skills in extracting and expressing key ideas.

- Example of stronger development: Studies in an appropriate environment. Keeps attention focused until the task is completed. Develops a personal strategy for extracting and relating ideas such as concept mapping, margin notes or "yellow stickies" to highlight main points of attention.

FINDING AND APPLYING RELEVANT EXAMPLES

- Example of weaker development: Expects to understand adequately by reading the preset material. Fails to see the learning value in examples. Fails to seek examples beyond those which are pre-selected in the study materials.

- Example of stronger development: Looks for examples from practice outside of course materials or framework. Deliberately tries to relate the examples to concepts in the study materials and to his or her own problem. Discards irrelevant examples but notices important points of transfer in relevant examples.

SELF-EVALUATION

- Example of weaker development: Cannot accurately predict how the instructor will evaluate his or her assignments or how he or she will do on the tests. Reacts to evaluation as a stressful, demotivating, and negative experience and may become ill or dysfunctional before a test or when having to hand in an assignment.

- Example of stronger development: Continuously looks at his or her own work in a critical but balanced way, noting its strengths and weaknesses relative to well-articulated criteria. Acts upon this continual self-analysis to improve weaknesses. Selects appropriate models of good and weak performance and uses these as points of reference for his or her own self-evaluation. Reflects upon what is expected in the course and by the instructor and extracts key ideas and criteria. Is not surprised by the final mark received in a course. Does not define the value of a course by the mark given by the instructor but by what he or she personally has learned from the experience.

Learning to Learn in Web-based Environments

Web-based environments can potentially offer students many more possibilities for enriching the learning process, compared to traditional course packages (Collis 1996, Khan 1997). Students can use a Web-based course environment for more communication opportunities, for more possibilities for collaboration and personal publishing, for more interaction with their instructors and classmates, and for access to a wider range of learning resources than was feasible before hyperlinked Web environments became conveniently available. Because Web-based environments offer nonlinear navigation of hyperlinked resources, the student, in theory, has at his or her fingertips not only all the materials of the course, but also a cyberlibrary of resources from all over the world, as well as contact possibilities with experts and fellow learners alike. It would seem that integrating a Web-based environment within a course should be an undoubted extension and enrichment to a course, and that having access to the WWW via a Web-based environment should clearly bring a wealth of new learning opportunities to the student. But such a conclusion overlooks an important filter to all these benefits—the capacity of the student to learn in such environments. This relates not only to his or her general maturity with respect to learning to learn, but also to new levels of complication about learning to learn that confront the student (and instructor) who makes use of Web-based opportunities. To illustrate this, we will make another list of the learning-to-learn components that we gave in the previous section, but this time indicate some of the new complications that affect learning to learn in Web-based environments.

LEARNING-TO-LEARN COMPONENTS:
ADDITIONAL CHALLENGES ARISING IN WEB-BASED ENVIRONMENTS

ARTICULATION AND REFLECTION

Web-based environments are new to the learner and require considerable learning in their own right. There are new concepts, new vocabulary, new browser options that all have to be learned. The attention that must be given to handling WWW tools and options presents concerns for the student that may make it harder for him or her to find the intellectual time and distance to reflect on the study material. If the student reflects at all, it is more likely to be about his or her learning curve in terms of using the WWW, instead of his or her learning curve in terms of the study material. Also, the technical aspects of Web-based environments may be unfamiliar to the student. He or she may be unable to articulate what is being experienced because of not knowing the terminology that relates WWW use. If the student is confused, he or she may not know enough about what to expect in Web-based environments to know how to describe the problem or deal with its causes.

PLANNING SKILLS

Planning requires an ability to decompose a task into a sequence of subtasks, and to make realistic estimates of the time and effort needed for each subtask. When working within new environments such as the WWW, the student has no base of experience on which to make such planning. How long should he or she predict that preparing a draft of a essay to be linked to a WWW site will take, for example? How much time will be taken up by unforeseen technical problems and deviations? How much time will be needed for searching the WWW, maintaining bookmarks, printing, file-management tasks, and recovering lost files? How much time will be needed for properly linking files and images via relative and external paths? To converting figures and formatting to forms appropriate to WWW publishing? And on top of this, as the student gains more opportunites to interact with others via Web-based environments, planning and maintaining tempo become increasingly complex, in that he or she becomes dependent on the planning and tempo-maintaining skills of others, often with very different contexts for their contribution to a common task.

STUDY SKILLS

While a student in higher education has had many years to develop his or her study skills and may be quite proficient at extracting and summarizing materials from a textbook or making notes at a lecture, the newness of Web-based environments means that new skills and procedures must be developed. New tools and terminology must be mastered in order to do something as simple as making a margin note. To many students, this may result in an unpleasant sense of incompetence and inefficiency.

FINDING AND APPLYING RELEVANT EXAMPLES

Hyperlinking to examples and related documents is one of the major strengths of the WWW. But also one of its most serious problems. There is so much available, published by anyone with the motivation to do so, that quality assessment and quantity filtering are being pushed onto the student, instead of being the responsibility of teams of professionals such as textbook authors and editors, and instructors. The student must sift through large numbers of examples, developing the wisdom and perception to select only those with the most meaningful application to his or her work. This is not only a new and complex responsibility for the student, but affects the effectiveness of his or her planning and the efficiency of his or her study habits. For many students confronted with the vastness of information and examples available through the WWW, the response is to not treat any of it as meaningful study material, because it is not the "real" textbook, and therefore not the basis of course examinations. WWW resources are rather like the "extra for experts" ideas at the end of a textbook chapter—obligatory for the author to provide, but of doubtful interest to the majority of task-focused students. We have found that many of our students appreciate using the WWW as a sort of treasure chest, but for small treasures such as new sources of buttons or images, or lists of references, not as real study material.

SELF-EVALUATION

If self-evaluation is difficult in both concept and technique in traditional study situations, it is even more difficult in an environment whose major strength is often defined by the choice of different resources and learning paths it offers the student. How can the instructor teach self-evaluation skills to students who are choosing different study materials and even different learning tasks? This creates a responsibility for one-to-one guidance of the student by the instructor, sometimes an impossible task logistically.

That these difficulties are encountered by our students when they use the WWW is not surprising. Compounding the difficulty even further is another aspect—determining a student's level of learning-to-learn skills related to the WWW. How we measure the starting point and the improvement in a student's learning-to-learn skills? Too often, we only know how to make test items that measure what the student has learned, not the process by which the student learned it. For example, Figure 2.1 shows the case of two hypothetical students who end up with the same score on a final test but in fact have different levels of development in their learning-to-learn skills. How do we test for this?

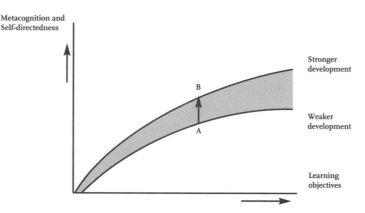

Figure 2.1. The Difference in Development Between Two Students

Student A reaches the same score on a test with respect to content acquisition as did Student B. Student B however experienced a stronger development in his/her learning-to-learn skills, such as self-directed planning.

HOW SHOULD INSTRUCTORS PROCEED?
HOW DO WE TEACH LEARNING TO LEARN IN WWW ENVIRONMENTS?

There are ways for instructors and designers of WWW-based courses to proceed. Young (1997) emphasizes that instructors can explicitly model learning-to-learn skills for their students and provide scaffolding for them as they practice these skills. Young defines *scaffolding* as a temporary instructional-support structure "designed to bridge the gap between what the student can accomplish independently and what the student can accomplish with guidance" (p. 41). Dunlap (1997) reviewed the literature on "life-long learning" skills, highly related to learning to learn, and identified four major sets of instructional strategies for the development of such skills and in particular of self-directedness:

- Students are given assignments that involve collaborative activities

- Students are helped to reflect about their work

- Students are given gradually increasing autonomy in terms of directing and planning

- Students are engaged in intrinsically motivating activities

Conversely, when students are not able to work effectively with these instructional strategies they may be candidates for weaker learning-to-learn development as shown in Figure 2.1. Collaboration can address the problem of unequal commitment among students and of a few persons telling the others what to do. Reflection can address articulation, reflection, and self-evaluation of work. Student autonomy may relate to study skills, planning, and finding appropriate examples. Intrinsically motivating activities can address the problem of students who are only extrinsically motivated by grades or tests.

We have been approaching the question of how to help students learn to learn in WWW-based courses from three directions: (1) by helping the student develop general learning-to-learn skills themselves for the WWW, (2) by shaping the instructional activities that make use of the WWW so that learning to learn is deliberately scaffolded, and (3) by designing the WWW-based environments to help in the learning-to-learn process. In the following section, we show how we are trying to develop these three perspectives in parallel, via the example of a first-year course in the design of educational media for students at the University of Twente, a course which makes extensive use of a Web-based environment within which the students must learn to learn.

The Case Study: Learning to Learn in Collaborative Groups in the WWW-based First-Year Course "ISM–1"

At the University of Twente in the Netherlands, first-year students in the Faculty of Educational Science and Technology follow the course "Instrumentatie Technologie 1" (ISM–1). These Dutch words can be translated as the "technology of learning instruments." In the theoretical portion of the course, students are introduced to the use and possibilities of media in education, and in the practical-activity portion of the course participate in three group projects in which they design and produce instructional video products, desktop-published brochures and different multimedia WWW sites using the programming language Java Script. The general goals of the course are:

- Content-related. To introduce students to major forms of educational media and to a model for the design and development of learning-related media products.

- Skill-related. To introduce students to the use of a broad range of professional tools for the design and production of educational media.

- Group-learning related. To help students work effectively and efficiently in a collaborative way as members of a learning group.

- Professional-development related. To initiate students into the professional community of educational media designers. To help them learn how to learn and work in such a community in an increasingly self-responsible way.

The course runs for the entire academic year. It is split into three cycles, one per trimester, and within each cycle the students participate in a different design-and-development project. In 1996–97 there were approximately seventy students in the course. (For a complete description, see Collis, Verhagen, Gervedink Nijhuis, and Meeuwsen, 1996.)

THE INTEGRATED WWW ENVIRONMENT FOR THE COURSE

The learning process in this course is supported by an integrated WWW-environment (URL: http://www.edte.utwente.nl/ism/ism1–96/home.htm). This site is used to integrate all aspects of the course experience: course organization, study and reference materials, support for all the group-process aspects of the course, and for all the communication aspects of the course. Figure 2.2 shows the homepage of the 1996–97 version of the course.

The navigation frame is the important "doorway" to the course environment and is always present in the same place on the screen for the students. The icons, from top to bottom, are links to:

the homepage

Project icons to move between the environments for the first, second, and third projects of the course

to the "First Stop" page, which the students must read at the start of the week. They must assume their own responsibility for this, getting into the habit of going to a computer and checking the First Stop every Monday morning. First Stop gives the overall view of all the week's activities

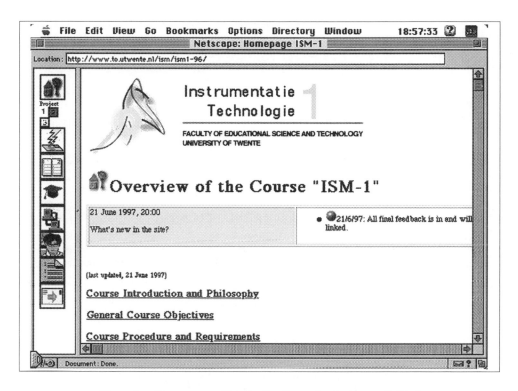

Figure 2.2. Homepage and Navigation Frame for the Course "ISM-1"

 to the "Week-by-Week" Center, in which the students see a more-detailed agenda for planning both the theoretical and practical aspects of the course

 to the "Study Center," where students find another organized set of links, this time to the hyperlinked study materials for each week and to the notes for the course lectures (there are five lectures per trimester)

 to the "Group Center," where students find all the information they need for their group projects

 to the "Specialist Center," where students find the specific resources they need to use the software tools needed in the group projects to the "Resource Center," where students find general-purpose support materials, such as a summary of the objectives of each week's study materials, a course glossary, and a summary of the "design guidelines" developed in the course

 to the "Communication Center", where students and instructors can conveniently send emails to one another

Figure 2.3. Shows the "Week-by-Week Center" with integrated "electronic agenda" for the course (in this example, during the first trimester).

SUPPORTING GROUP-BASED COLLABORATIVE LEARNING VIA THE WWW ENVIRONMENT

A critical aspect of the development of learning how to learn in the course is the use of the "Jigsaw Method," (Aronson *et al*, 1978) in which each student in a group is responsible for particular tasks. Figure 2.4 shows a list of students in one of the eight groups of the course, with the roles they have chosen.

In each group there are students with the same task, who must work together across the

Figure 2.3. The WEEK-by-WEEK Center.
The study materials and the instructions for the assignments are integrated here.

Figure 2.4. Students and Their Particular Task

The WWW site lets all students and the instructors easily see who the members of each group are and what particular roles they have. Links to the role names brings up the detailed responsibilities for each role.

groups to help each other, as well as make their unique contribution to their own group. The Specialist Center is where the students with the same roles, but in different groups, can find resources to help themselves and each other (Figure 2.5).

Students identify strongly with their groups, and use the Web-based Group Center in the course site not only for support of their collaboration, but also to display their work to themselves and to the other groups. Figure 2.6 shows the Group Center and Figure 2.7 shows a part of the Planning Page for an individual group, pages which are entered via the Group Center.

An important part of the learning-to-learn experience in the course is the emphasis on self-responsibility for planning and the staying on tempo. We give explicit expectations for what is due each week, but give the students considerable freedom on when, where, and how they do it. In general, students arrange their own work, and no instructor is present. All instructions and examples are available via the WWW site, but students must take the effort and initiative to locate the resources in the site and decide how best to make use of them. Most of the resources are written by us specifically for the course, but many are links

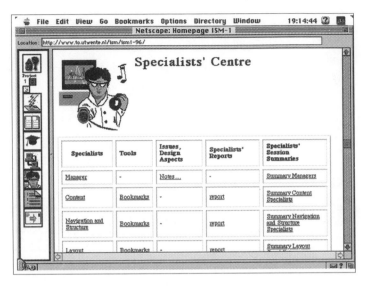

Figure 2.5. The Specialist Center.

Each specialist has their own responsibilities—these responsibilities,
and help to carry them out, are linked in the Specialist Center.

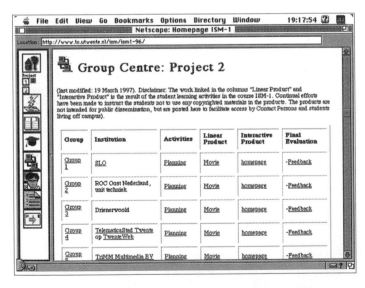

Figure 2.6. The Group Center at the End of the Second Project

All final results are available to the entire group and to the outside world.

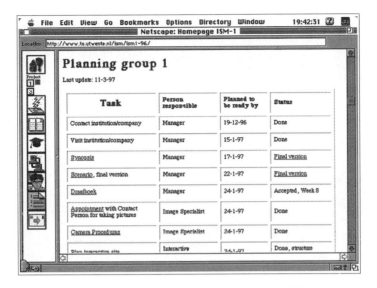

Figure 2.7. The Planning Page for One of the Groups

The planning page is used to support collaboration with explicit responsibilities for each student.

to external WWW sites. In this way, we try to scaffold the students into the habit of making selective use of a library of possibilities. Figure 2.8 shows the bookmark page from the Specialist Center for Project 3 for the HTML-JavaScript specialists from each group.

SUPPORTING LEARNING TO LEARN FROM HYPERLINKED STUDY MATERIALS

In order to emphasize to the students that the theoretical and practical aspects of the course are tightly integrated, and also to give them the experience of learning via hyperlinked materials, we have written all the study materials and placed them on the WWW site. Figure 2.9 shows the Study Center for Project 2 in which the links to the study materials and lecture notes relate to the different phases of the group activities that the students are experiencing in each given week.

During the 1997–98 course cycle we are adding self-quizzes to the study materials, taking advantage of the increasing interactivity available on the WWW. We hope that these self-test options will help the learning-to-learn process for the students. We are also adding more links to examples that illustrate points in the study materials in order to help

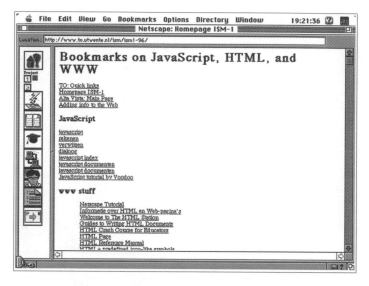

Figure 2.8. A Bookmark Collection, Study Resources,
and Example Materials for Learning HTML and JavaScript

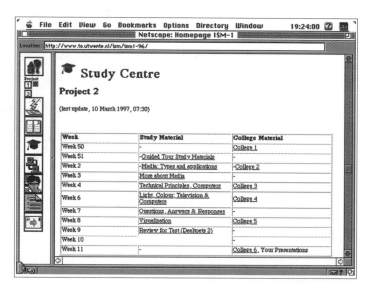

Figure 2.9. The Study Center With Links to Hyperlinked Study Materials
(Note: "College" is Dutch for "Lecture")

students better develop the learning-to-learn skill related to making good use of models and examples. To support this process for ourselves, we are studying many examples of WWW-based courses to see how others are approaching the scaffolding process, either explicitly or implicitly (Winnips 1997).

EVALUATION AS A KEY LEARNING-TO-LEARN COMPONENT

We believe that self- and peer evaluations are critical to the development of learning to learn in our course (see Collis and Meeuwsen 1997). Through frequent use of self- and peer evaluations, we are trying to transform the meaning of the term *evaluation* for the students to be not a judgmental moment at the end of the course when the instructor imparts a label on the student's work, but a constructive, ongoing process within the course through which students learn how to efficiently and effectively articulate the strengths and weaknesses of their own work, as a basis for improvement. As criteria for this ongoing evaluation, an important conceptual link between the study materials and the group projects are the design guidelines. These are sets of rules for good practice that are introduced in each set of study materials (approximately twenty per trimester), and that the students must apply in many ways in their projects. We have a number of ways to use the WWW to support self- and peer evaluation based on these design guidelines. Figure 2.10 shows how we make sure that the students know that the criteria they will used on their self- and peer evaluations are precisely the criteria that were developed in their study materials. Because all the study materials are available in the site, students can easily link back to the Design Guidelines to refresh their memories of what the guidelines indicate.

Figure 2.11 shows how we use CGI forms to make evaluation based on the design guidelines as easy as possible to carry out for the students, and for us to collect as the instructors.

The students' evaluative comments are important to our process and are linked to the course site (as well as our own). We explicitly build on those comments, for example, by linking the final grade for the project work to how carefully the students have taken into account the suggestions made by their peers for improving their products. Thus we ask them to explicitly react to the peer evaluations and explain how they revised their products based on these suggestions. The WWW site makes everything available to everyone, so there is no problem with keeping track of all these suggestions. Figure 2.12 shows part of a planning page for a group, in which the links to the forms for instructor, group, and peer evaluation are shown, and the links to the entries made via those forms are also given.

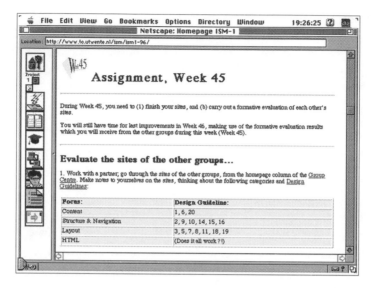

Figure 2.10. Design Guidelines are Used to Support Both the Self-Evaluation and the Peer-Evaluations.

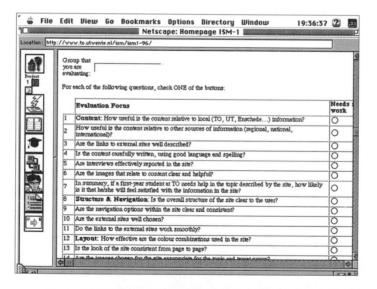

Figure 2.11. CGI Forms Make the Evaluation More Structured

The forms shows how we use CGI Forms to make evaluation based on the design guidelines as easy as possible to carry out for the students, and for us to collect as the instructors.

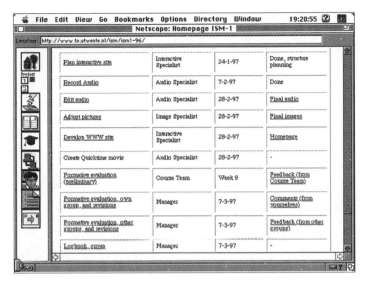

**Figure 2.12. A Group Planning Page, Showing How the Various Evaluation Moments
are Organized and Their Results Linked Directly to the Page**

COMMUNICATION AS A LEARNING-TO-LEARN TOOL

There are a variety of forms of communication supported by the WWW, all of which have different contributions to the learning-to-learn process. One-to-many communication occurs via First Stop, where students must develop their own self-responsibility to read the instructions for the week. One-to-one communication is used when the instructors wish to provide personalized guidance and support, and when the students want to ask for help. In the latter case, we urge the students to first ask each other, and only as a last resort to ask their instructors, in order to develop more self-reliant study habits. Figure 2.13 shows a portion of the Communication Center for the course, in which every message can be sent to any particular student or member of the course team.

Also, as we have shown in examples above, we make consistent use of CGI forms for structured communication, and in turn integrate the students' entries into these forms into the course site. This we hope helps to develop a sense of intrinsic motivation for the reflection process—the student's own self-reflection will become a valued part of the study environment of the course. Figure 2.14 shows one such reflection, from one of the

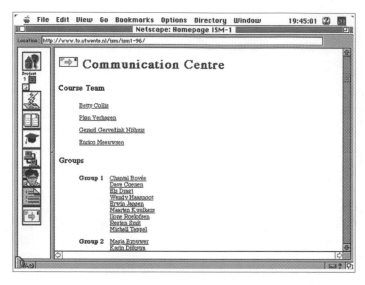

Figure 2.13. The Communication Center encourages Students
to Ask Each Other for Help Before Asking the Course Team

Managers in Project 2. All the Managers in each of the groups keep such a reflective journal, available via a link from each group's planning page.

Learning to Learn in WWW Environments: What s Next?

This first-year course, fully integrated in a Web environment which grew to many thousands of pages and files, has been successfully completed by almost all of the first-year
students, on time, and with good results. We believe that we have incorporated a number
of features to help the students learn how to learn in WWW environments. But we also
know we still have much to learn ourselves. The technology continually changes, thus
presenting us all with new learning tasks just to handle it. Issues relating to helping
students plan and organize their time are a major source of concern to us, in that the
approach we now use requires a great deal of instructor structuring and monitoring.
Stimulating students to not study for the test but for their own professional development
is a continual challenge.

In conclusion, learning to learn is a complex, gradually developed set of skills and

Figure 14. Beginning of a Manager's Journal, Kept as a Week-to-Week Reflective
Report and Linked to the Course Site

orientations, difficult to measure, difficult to teach or to scaffold, and highly influenced by
personal characteristics such as self-esteem and even wisdom. Given a new technical environment, and immediate access to a virtually unlimited amount of both filtered and unfil-
tered information and human contacts, learning to learn now faces an additional layer of
challenges—how can we help students to learn how to learn, effectively and efficiently, in
a WWW-based environment? Just as learning to learn is a never completed process for the
learner, setting up and managing instructional settings for such learning are also never-
completed processes for the instructor.

References

Aronson, E., Blaney, N. Stephan, C. Sikes, J., and Snapp, M. 1978. *The Jigsaw Classroom.* (Beverly Hills, CA: Sage).

Collis, B. 1996.*Tele-Learning in a Digital World: The Future of Distance Learning.* (London: International Thomson Publications.

Collis, B., and Meeuwsen, E. 1997. *New Approaches to Evaluation Via the WWW.* Presentation at the Seminar "Tele-Learning at the University of Twente," 31 January 1997. (http://www.edte.utwente.nl/user/collis/presents/eval-ism.htm)

Collis, B., Verhagen, P., Gervedink Nijhuis G., and Meeuwsen, E. 1996. "Learning From Experience: An Interim Evaluation of the Course ISM–1 at the University of Twente." Internal Report, Faculty of Educational Science and Technology, University of Twente. (http://www.edte.utwente.nl/user/ism/Collis/papers/ismdec96.htm)

Dunlap, J. 1997. "Preparing Students for Lifelong Learning: A Review of Instructional Methodologies." Paper presented at the Annual Meeting of the AECT, Albuquerque, NM.

Khan, B. (Ed.). 1997. *Web-based Instruction.* (Englewood Cliffs, NJ: Educational Technology Publications).

Winnips, K. 1997. "Scaffolding in WWW-based Courses." Internal report, faculty of Educational Science and Technology, University of Twente (http://utto212. utwente.nl/scaffolding.htm).

Young, A. C. 1997. "Higher-order Learning and Thinking: What Is It and How Is It Taught?" *Educational Technology,* 37 (4), 38–41.

Augmenting Traditional Teaching with Internet-based Options

Steve Bett, Deanie French, Gerald Farr, and Lori Hooks

Learning to harness Internet resources does not require you to become an expert in computers, networking, advanced multimedia technologies or programming. You do not need to be an expert in computers or networking to use the Internet any more than you need to be a mechanic to drive a car. In either situation, the expert knowledge you pick up along the way may help, but it is not a requirement. Just as with cars, you will need to seek out an expert when you have a technical problem or question. Once you identify your objective, then others can help you find talent on your campus or in your company to help you achieve it. Rather than providing technical details, this chapter presents a selection of inspirational ideas from just a few of the many educators now augmenting their teaching through Web-based resources.

Both teachers and learners must adapt to new styles of teaching and learning to meet future learning requirements. Steve Bett (1994) noted that colleges need to help students cope with these new learning environments and conditions in a productive manner. "To do this, there needs to be more emphasis on process; how to learn, retool, update, communicate, and less on content. Teaching can be content rich but the emphasis should be on process." Bett further adds, "it is no longer cost effective to focus just on the 'facts' which are true today but may take on new meanings tomorrow."

The following presents a range of methods for augmenting traditional courses with Internet elements as a prelude to the subsequent examples of how educators from a wide range of disciplines have imaginatively intergrated the Net in their teaching.

INTEGRATING ONLINE WEB-BASED OPTIONS

1. *Syllabus*. Online syllabi have been widely adopted because they simplify the distribution and updating of these documents.

2. *Lecture notes*. Many educators are expanding traditional lectures through lecture notes online. If the teacher desires to limit access to the notes to those who are officially registered in the course, the notes can be password protected.

3. *Discussion*. In-class questioning and discussion is a traditional feature of a college course. The Internet provides a way of extending the discussion and answer period beyond the fifty minute class period. We have found that the practice of posting questions and answers about specific topics can enhance the quality of interchange. Students who typically take longer to formulate their questions and students who are reluctant to speak up in class will generally participate online.

4. *Office hours via e-mail*. E-mail extends teacher/student interaction. E-mail in lieu of a scheduled office hour is a great convenience for the student and the teacher because it is not schedule dependent. Students send e-mail when it is convenient for them while the teacher replies after devoting time to carefully consider the question.

5. *Online term paper*. When students know that their papers are going to be published online, they typically put more effort into the project and do a better job. Online papers—particularly papers that the student is allowed to re-write, can benefit from the comments of peers as well as the teacher. To some extent this lessens the teacher's task of catching the problems related to exposition and factual errors. The teacher no longer has to be the sole evaluator.

6. *Collaborative conferencing systems*. Networked collaboration skills are being highly prized by

organizations. Teamwork is enhanced through such systems as Lotus Notes and the German-based public system, Basic Support for Cooperative Work (BSCW) are reviewed in Chapter 4, "Skills for Developing, Utilizing and Evaluating Internet-based Alternatives."

7.   *Testing*. Practice tests can be provided online to help students master course content. Faculty may want to consider using sample tests or older parallel tests for a mid-term or final. Many faculty use in-class or other types of proctored exams for grade determination.

8.   *Tutorials*. Current software makes it easy to develop slideshow tutorials. Online tutorials on the use of e-mail, search techniques, and other foundation skills are becoming increasingly available.

Examples of Web-Based Learning Across Disciplines

Many professors and instructors are taking advantage of the Internet to varying degrees to augment and support their course content. In some instances, the "medium is the message," such as in technology and education classes. In others, the instructor is merely using the Internet as a means to disseminate information to students. Whether it is posting items that previously required reams of paper (such as lengthy assignments and syllabi), or linking to the latest daily press release or stock information in business or finance classes, the use of the Internet offers new ways for educators to enhance the classroom experience.

This chapter provides innovative real world examples of Web-based course pages. Visit as many as you can, and you will find how different uses of links, library resources, sound files, and discussion groups, have been utilized by other teachers.

WORLD LECTURE HALL

The University of Texas sponsored site called World Lecture Hall (see figure 3.1) is a good place to start searching for examples by discipline. There are hundreds of sites to review—we have included only a few here. If you wish to see how others in your field have used Internet-based resources, visit this site frequently. You will find examples of course syllabi, assignments, lecture notes, exams, class calendars, multimedia textbooks, and other uses of the Internet for the classroom. There is a "What's New" feature to view the most recent additions.

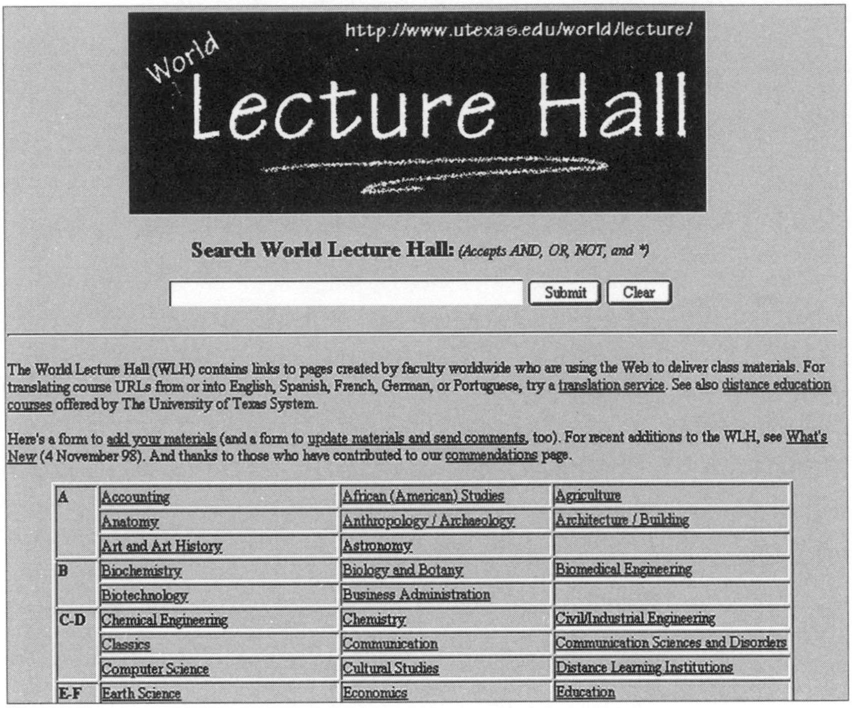

Figure 3.1 World Lecture Hall at the University of Texas

http://www.utexas.edu/world/lecture/

ART HISTORY 185 AT POMONA COLLEGE

http://pom-mac2.pomona.edu/classes/syllabus/arthi185.html

The site features an extensive online syllabus, with course assignments and activities outlined in detail. There are also links to the homepages of various local exhibits (class activities include visiting these art exhibits) and reading assignments. Since the syllabus clearly states that attendance is mandatory, this site is a supplemental resource for students to facilitate study and preparation before class time.

BIOLOGY 100/101 AT THE UNIVERSITY OF ILLINOIS AT URBANA CHAMPAIGN

http://www.life.uiuc.edu/bio100/

Students can preview course information, including lab guidelines, exam review information, and lecture syllabus. There are links to other life science resource sites, and extra credit assignments are posted. Most interesting is the use of the "Virtual Cell," which gives students the opportunity to study the parts of a cell right at their own computer. Link to the "Virtual Cell," and follow the online tutorial for an effective example of how Internet technology takes textbook illustration one step further (see figure 3.2).

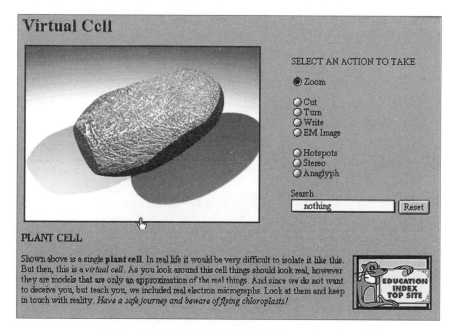

Figure 3.2   Virtual Cell

BIOLOGY 1410 AT SOUTHWEST TEXAS STATE UNIVERSITY

http://www.study.swt.edu

Students use Web-based lecture slides to review lecture content (see figure 3.3). After presentation of the information in class, students can review key concepts by logging into the Internet when they return home. Links to Web sites that support and augment the topic are included below the slides. Each page provides an e-mail link to the professor for ready communication of questions about the topic. For students who do not have Web access, there is hard copy in the library of the lecture notes presented in class.

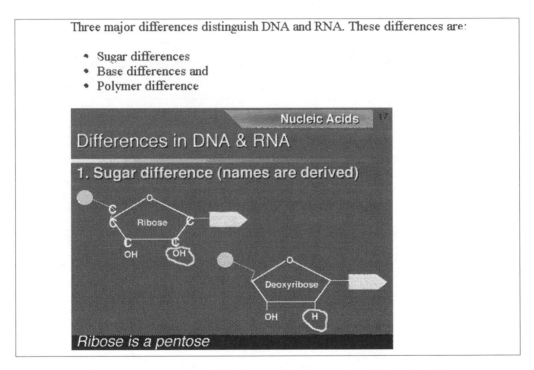

Figure 3.3 Internet-based Slide Presented in Class and Available on the Web

COMMUNICATION 201 AT CORNELL UNIVERSITY

http://instruct1.cit.cornell.edu/courses/comm201e/

This site features a public speaking course with an online component that takes advantage of Netscape sound (.wav) files to make audio examples of famous speeches available to all students. Students may review these speeches as many times as they wish, providing them with concrete examples of a variety of communication styles.

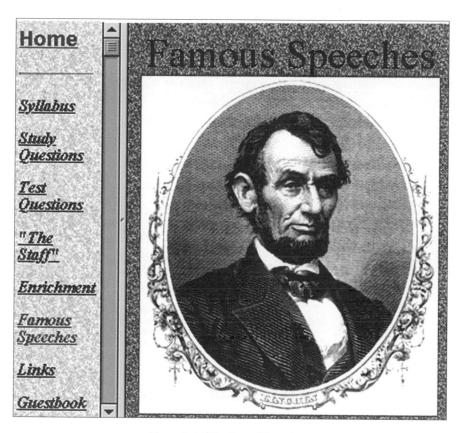

Figure 3.4 Collection of Speeches

THE CROSSROADS PROJECT

http://www.georgetown.edu/crossroads/about.html

The American Studies Electronic Crossroads (ASEC) involves four areas of activity: (1) Pedagogical, scholarly, and institutional information for the international American Studies Community, along with full information about the American Studies Association; (2) Experimental projects of curriculum revision in key American Studies courses at different test sites, and by individual faculty members who are using electronic media as newly integrated tools in the American Studies curriculum; (3) Creation of workbooks, videotapes, disks, and other materials intended to assist teachers and students in making use of technology and in promoting international collaboration in the study of American history and culture; and (4) Sponsorship of a series of workshops and institutes at the national and regional levels to foster serious innovation in American Studies curricula especially related to the integration of new technologies, as well as electronic literacy and other aspects of faculty development.

This site is most interesting to explore as it contains many valuable ideas.

Figure 3.5   The Crossroads Project

ENGLISH. AMBIVALENCE IN AMERICAN THOUGHT AND LETTERS AT ABT. ANGLISTIK/AMERIKANISTIK, HUMBOLDT-UNIVERSITY

http://userpage.fu-berlin.de/~mayer/ambivlnz/index.htm

This site examines the theme of ambivalence as an historical principle with links to six major works of American literature and a variety of secondary works.

Figure 3.6   Examination of the Theme of Ambivalence

EXERCISE PHYSIOLOGY AT NORTHERN ARIZONA UNIVERSITY

http://www.nau.edu:80/~hp/proj/rah/courses/exs336/exs336.html

This site utilizes the homepage to post syllabi, lecture outlines, and sample test questions. It also contains information on related newsgroups for the student's use and a web tutorial. The instructor has also posted a page of recommended journals found on campus to help with research projects.

FINANCE: AN INTEGRATED PERSONAL PLANNING APPROACH
AT THE UNIVERSITY OF DAYTON

http://udayton.edu/sba/wf/pf.htm

This is a companion site to a text. The authors sponsor this site for use in their own classes and as a preformatted website for any faculty who utilize their book. This site features Internet exercises as supplements to the text, spreadsheet templates for use in class, and links to resources on the Internet. PowerPoint presentations are posted here for other faculty to use. This type of support for textbooks and accessibility to the authors may be the new wave in textbook publishing.

GENETICS AT NORTH DAKOTA STATE UNIVERSITY

http://www.ndsu.nodak.edu/instruct/mcclean/plsc431/

This site posts each topic by class schedule. Students can access each posting for reading before class. The instructor has also posted study questions to help students prepare for each quiz.

HEALTH PROMOTION: 96:218 NURSING OF CHILDREN AT IOWA UNIVERSITY

http://www.nursing.uiowa.edu

According to Jan Denely, RN, Ph.D. at Iowa University:

We use electronic media in our classroom, and use e-mail for student announcements and discussion. Students are expected to be computer literate—some drag their feet, others knock your socks off with their projects. We do a web page at the end of the class to share the student projects done over the semester—these are graduate students in Child Health Nursing. Last year's class web page has been put down as a favorite on a few of the school nursing pages—it has also resulted in numerous contacts from all over the country (each student's e-mail number is at the end of their page). Some of the contacts resulted in one student doing a chapter in an upcoming textbook, a number being invited to do programs—one will be a keynote in Montana—one was asked to sell the computer rights to her work (we said "no"). This year's class is much smaller, but you can look at our content-oriented (not glitzy) web page.

MATH. BUSINESS STATISTICS AT ARKANSAS STATE UNIVERSITY

http://www.clt.astate.edu/jseydel/qm2113.htm

Concepts and uses of data analysis for supporting decision-making are described in this site. There are many online examples. This site integrates Excel and SPSS for downloading homework with computational support, primarily in the area of descriptive statistics. Syllabus, assignments, exams, grades are linked to related materials. Students are encouraged to make use of e-mail and listserv options. Emphasis is placed on the need for learner involvement in the learning process.

MEDIA VOICES, MEDIA STYLE AT SWINBURNE UNIVERSITY, AUSTRALIA

http://www.swin.edu.au/ssb/media/am209/wwwbopax/wwwboard.html

This site contains a message board, e-mail to the teacher and weekly outlines and teaching materials. Of particular interest are the links to hot and current media topics and the Web discussion section, which is an open forum for students to post comments regarding the course content, current events, or readings. This lays the groundwork for face to face discussion during class time, and makes the Web resources vital to group participation.

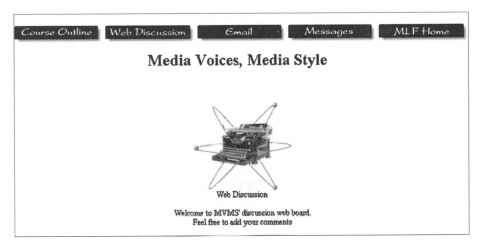

Figure 3.7 Web Discussion System

METAPHYSICS HOME PAGE AT NORTHWEST MISSOURI STATE UNIVERSITY

http://www.nwmissouri.edu/~rfield/570home.html

This site links the class syllabus, helpful writing guidelines, and a variety of Internet resources for students enrolled in the class. The Internet resources are mostly online encyclopedias and biographical resources on the Internet and are designed to familiarize students with these types of resources.

NURSING-PEDIATRIC. BAND-AIDES AT COLUMBIA UNIVERSITY

http://funrsc.fairfield.edu/~jfleitas/contents.html

According to Joan Fleitas, who developed this site as part of her doctoral dissertation at Columbia University:

> This is a site about growing up with medical problems . . . any ole type. Its goal is to help people understand what it's like, from the perspective of the children and teens who are doing just that. These kids

have become experts at coping with problems that most children have never heard of. They'd like you to know how they do it, and they hope that you'll be glad you came to visit. I've divided the contents into three ponds: one for kids, one for teens, and one for adults. Figure out which you are, and jump in.

Any discipline that works with children will find this site a must see to obtain ideas for teaching students how to develop child-centered Web pages. The unusual characters for links and immediate interaction make this a model site for emulation. The concepts in this site can be easily adapted to adult format. Fleitas's Band-Aides site is the winner of many awards.

Figure 3.8 Jump Right In

NURSING-PEDIATRIC AT COLUMBIA UNIVERSITY. AN EXAMPLE OF AN ONLINE TOUR

http://funrsc.fairfield.edu/~jfleitas/julia1.html

Even though Dr. Fleitas uses this site for pediatric nursing, it is a model for integrating the "human element" into the technological processes. The tour idea can be easily adapted to wide range of activities where participants need reassurance or emotional support.

This site features a hospital tour by Julia, a patient, describing why she is in the hospital: "Hello! My name is Julia. I came to the hospital because I had seizures. They were caused by a tumor in my brain. A tumor is something that doesn't cooperate with all of the other parts of the brain. So it was good to get it removed. I was a little nervous when I came to the hospital, but that was OK. I am nine years old; old enough to learn that there are a lot of good things about the hospital. I think that you'll agree with me, if you stick around."

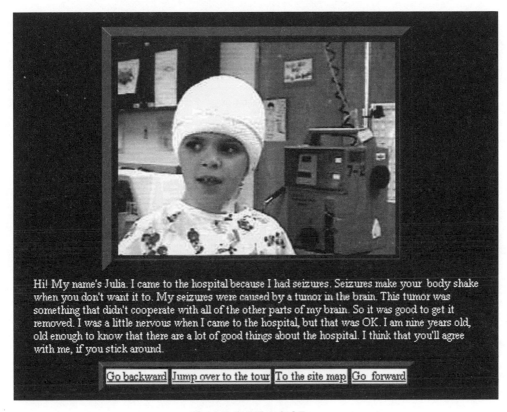

Figure 3.9 A Hospital Tour

PHYSICS 211 AT THE UNIVERSITY OF KENTUCKY

http://www.pa.uky.edu/~phy211/index.html

This site provides JAVA applet exercises for students, as well as example lab setup photos.

SOCIOLOGY: LINKING TWO COUNTRIES

http://vc.lemoyne.edu/

This site is a virtual classroom for a sociology course. In fall 1997, Raymond Bucko, S.J. taught "Social Theory in Sociology and Anthropology" using BSCW (Basic Support for Cooperative Work) as well as a private newsgroup for enhanced asynchronous classroom participation. In spring 1998, Le Moyne College in Syracuse, New York, in conjunction with the University of Deusto, Bilbao, in the Basque Country in Spain will offer cooperatively a course using BSCW as its workspace program for creating a shared virtual classroom environment. Students from each school will use the workspace to share and discuss ideas relevant to the course.

Visitors are encouraged to view Le Moyne College's online Web Authoring Tutorials, an ongoing effort to promote Internet Assisted Teaching and Communication at their institution.

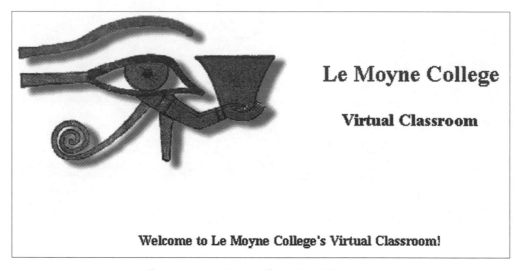

Figure 3.10 Le Moyne College Virtual Classroom

STRATEGIC MANAGEMENT AT UNIVERSITY AT ALBANY, SUNY SCHOOL OF BUSINESS

http://www.albany.edu/~pm157/teaching/mgt682.html

This site, a graduate course homepage, features many valuable links for students. The instructor has integrated course topics with current online resources such as commercial sites, news articles and reviews, Lexis/Nexis, and research articles from other universities. This approach allows the students to utilize both traditional textbook readings, and up-to-the minute Web-based readings. When it comes to staying on top of trends in business, you can't get any more current than this approach.

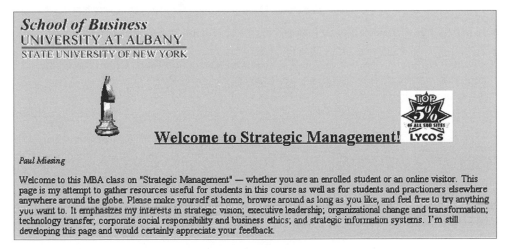

Figure 3.11 Strategic Management

Conclusion

This chapter provides many ideas to stimulate thought about content which would be appropriate for migration to Internet formats. Once you have an idea of what you would like to accomplish, become proactive and find those in the university or business setting who can help you obtain the minimal skills to get it online. The good news is that any document created by mainstream, current version word processing software, can be saved as an HTML document (converting text and graphics into HTML files understood by Web browsers). The bad news is that while this simple conversion is good for syllabi and other course information, too many educators convert entire manuscripts for students to read online. The lecture in front of the class becomes the lecture online. Information on the Web should be in much smaller units with hyperlinks to other sites when appropriate.

Chapter 4, "Skills for Developing, Utilizing and Evaluating Internet-based Alternatives," will provide tools to help you develop material to augment lectures and build Internet-based resources. You should find comfort in the fact that every year the development of Internet-based materials becomes easier as software companies find ways to let us communicate in new media with the minimum amount of technical expertise.

References

Bett, Steve (1994). "Envisioning a Center for Learning Technologies," unpublished paper presented to the School of Education, University of Louisville.

DeMott, Kenneth (1996). "Evaluation of Computer Assisted Instruction Using Criteria based on Principles of Learning Theory" (Online). Available at http://parsons.ab.umd.edu/~kdemott/pages/eval.html

Skills for Developing, Utilizing and Evaluating Internet-based Learning

Deanie French

This chapter presents progressively more sophisticated ways to integrate Web-based technology with your current teaching methods. Six skill areas are presented to assist you in becoming technologically enabled for Internet-based design.

1. Interpersonal relationships through electronic networking

2. Harvesting the Internet for instructional resources

3. Assessment of Web sites

4. Integrating the Web in teaching through self-directed modules.

5. Integrating elements with an interactive course manager

6. Utilizing collaborative conferencing systems.

Interpersonal Relationships through Electronic Networking

One of the most important concepts to appreciate is the fact that the Internet not only links computers to computers, but more importantly it links people to people.

According to Agre (1997) in "Networking on the Net": "Several million people employ electronic mail for some significant portion of their professional communications. Yet, in my experience, few people have figured out how to use the net productively. " In this paper, available at http://communication.ucsd.edu/pagere/network.html, Agre offers some excellent tips:

1. Don't treat people impersonally.

2. Remember that being polite is basic to effective interactions.

3. Follow-up on e-relationships. Forward items of interest to your contacts.

4. Thank anyone who helps you obtain information.

5. Promote your own work, but keep it low-key.

6. Use electronic networking as a part of the larger ecology of communication.

7. Try different types of e-relationships. However, don't substitute them for human contact.

8. Maintain steady network building interactions.

9. Continually improve and evolve existing methods of networking.

10. Use the electronic media to not only enhance careers, but also to contribute to the vision of building a community.

E-MAIL SKILLS

The exchange of business cards is a time-honored tradition to enhance and to remember interpersonal relationships. Almost all of today's business cards include an e-mail address. Effective communication can no longer be limited to the telephone, the mail, and the fax machine. Increasingly individuals expect an e-mail answer in response to questions within hours rather days.

If you have never used e-mail for training or education, you should first become comfortable with a system. Once you feel comfortable, you are ready for augmenting your teaching methodology with e-mail. Netscape mail, and many other programs, lets you create individual folders to collect individual responses from students in a particular class (or any predefined group). I use this feature with my totally online course to maintain a copy of all the correspondence between the students and me in a single folder.

As you read your e-mail answer it immediately by using the reply button. If you don't reply after you read the message, you pay a costly price in terms of time to reopen and reread it before sending a reply. Many people don't read their mail online and print out all their messages, making an immediate reply impossible. It is good practice to learn how to read e-mail online so that you can respond promptly. Of course, there will be cases when you will want to reflect before answering. However, at least 90 percent of my e-mail can be answered immediately. If I need time to get more information, I acknowledge the receipt of the message immediately because e-mail has created the expectation of a rapid response.

I use an e-mail feature called an electronic e-mail distribution list that allows me to write one message and distribute it electronically to all members of my class. In an academic setting, the class roll can be easily converted to a distribution list. In industry, you may want to build your distribution by department, team, or function. The time spent setting this up is repaid in subsequent efficiency. Your company or academic computing center can also help you set up a listserv (described below) to handle large volumes of e-mail.

EMOTICONS AND ABBREVIATIONS

You will also encounter, and may want to use, emoticons and abbreviations. *Emoticons* are symbols used to help clarify the author's tone or intention in e-mail, chat rooms, listservs, bulletin boards, or electronic communication. They are not always appropriate in business e-mail. The following are a few examples;

:)	smile
: (	sadness
;)	wink
: 0	surprise
LOL	laughing out loud
ROFL	rolling on the floor laughing
IMHO	in my humble opinion
BTW	by the way

Other emoticons and abbreviations can be easily found at the following site: http://www.enternet.com.au/techno/emoticons.html

CHATROOMS

For my online course, I am currently trying a freeware system, WebChat Broadcasting System (WBS): http://pages.wbs.net/webchat3.so? WBS is the largest interactive and event network on the Web with 2.2 million registered users. According to its creators, more than 4,000 registrants are added every day. You should visit this site and explore its components for yourself. You do have to join before you can begin chatting. It is a fairly simple process. You join by e-mail, receive a verification number, and acknowledge its receipt. You then gain full access for chatting. You can even set up a private "room" for yourself and your invited audience. In private rooms, you establish the time of day you want to meet so participants can join you in real-time communication. An advantage of Internet Chat over other forms of conferencing is that, regardless of a participant's location you incur no long-distance charges. You do have to allow for time zones to insure everyone meets at the right time.

In a chat room, members may assume fictitious names or handles. Anonymity can safeguard you from unwanted e-mail. It is just safe practice to protect yourself by not revealing too much about yourself or taking others at face value.

To give you an example, as I love scuba diving, my first chat room handle was "Mermaid," which attracted unwanted requests to meet in private rooms for adult conversation. My new chat room handle is "Grandma" or "SWT Professor. " It is not unknown in public chat rooms for men to assume the role of women, women the role of men, teens the role of adults and for backgrounds to be invented. In my private class chat room, I expect real names and honest communication. Students realize that classroom interaction is very different from public chatrooms. Sophisticated chat rooms offer a block feature to keep anyone not invited from entering a particular chat room.

Chat rooms can be dramatic because they involve people sharing information about themselves. Several years ago in a patient education classroom, as part of a student demo, we visited the chat room for those interested in Twelve-Step programs. The night we visited was a harrowing experience for all of us when we encountered a participant in deep despair and on the verge of suicide. I share this example to illustrate the intimacy of chat rooms and e-mail. Even though the messages are electronic, the human emotions, reactions, and feelings are real. My students tend to use the chat room as one method for "bonding" as a team. They laugh and share lighthearted information, as well as serious class-related information.

CONNECTING THROUGH ELECTRONIC GROUP MAILING LISTS (LISTSERVS)

As Chapter 5 describes, a listserv opens electronic doors giving people access to content of common interest via e-mail. At first this process seems a little confusing. To fully understand, you should join at least three lists to compare differences in content and frequency of messages. Some lists generate more messages than you want to read. If this happens, try another. However, the quality of the list or information may offer enough value for you to want to stay subscribed and just delete messages on irrelevant topics. You quickly learn to scan messages for relevant content. Don't let messages engulf your life. You have to be receiving value for the time you spend. I have often unsubscribed from lists I have found unproductive. No one is offended if you don't stay on. There are a few terms that you may want to learn before joining a listserv.

> *Lurking* (participant activity): Just looking at the messages. Most people spend a lot of time just lurking until they are comfortable.
>
> *Spamming* (content of message): The equivalent of junk mail.
>
> *Flaming* (content of message): A hostile message—someone forgot that the message was being sent to an individual.

One of my favorite listservs is the Discussion Group for Training and Development (TRDEV-L) that is mentioned in chapter five. The information is as valuable for those in education as in business. I regularly use this list to gather information for several healthcare human resources classes. Despite the large amount of mail received from this list, the frequent nuggets of valuable resources and information make it a must for me. I've found that this group of peers frequently can provide just the exact resource I need. Directions for subscribing from the TRDEV-L site are as follows. Send e-mail to *LISTSERV@ LISTS.PSU.EDU* with the following, and only the following, in the body of the message:SUBSCRIBE TRDEV-L *your name* (e.g. Deanie French). You will receive an e-mail from the Listserv confirming your subscription within 48 hours and at which point you begin to receive mail.

BULLETIN BOARDS (INFORMATION SHARING)

There are two types of bulletin board systems (BBS): information bulletin systems and interactive systems. *Information bulletin boards* direct you to other sites. An example of such a board is "Howdy and Welcome to Aggieland – Jim Segers. "

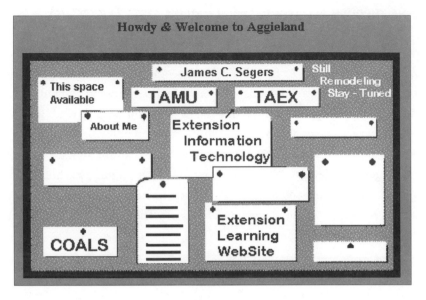

Figure 4.1
http://leviathan.tamu.edu:70/ctg/jsegers/jsegers.html

1st District Democrats BBS

Below is the 1st District Democrats BBS. You may need to hit reload after entering your message to see it appear here.

[Post Message] [FAQ]

- Information on Kay O'Conner - **Scott Benson** *14:15:22 4/08/97* (0)
- Washington Days - **Glenn Staab** *23:01:45 2/17/97* (0)
- Johnson County Democrats - **Micheline Burger** *16:23:50 2/12/97* (2)
  - Re: Johnson County Democrats - Promote Protect Our Democracy Network (**D. Stryker**) *19:52:32 5/13/97* (0)
  - Re: Johnson County Democrats - Promote Protect Our Democracy Network (**D. Stryker**) *19:52:03 5/13/97* (0)
- Johnson County Democrats - **Micheline Burger** *16:23:27 2/12/97* (0)
- Johnson Co. URL - **Bob Steinert** *08:10:43 1/30/97* (0)
- Happy New Year - **Calvin Rees** *07:06:51 1/01/97* (0)
- I need the results in the 115 House race - **Corey Olemon** *17:44:57 11/16/96* (0)
- Great Job - **Stan Fowler** *16:10:06 7/26/96* (0)
- District Map - **Terry Stroth** *22:34:13 6/17/96* (0)
- this is cool ! - **alice lieberman** *09:07:35 4/12/96* (0)
- Kansas Democratic Computer Caucus - **Calvin Rees** *08:57:05 4/08/96* (0)
- Greetings from a homesick Kansan! - **Mary Isenhour** *20:11:16 3/24/96* (0)
- New message board for all to use - **Calvin Rees** *15:25:38 3/22/96* (0)
- New BBS - **Steven K. Buehler** *14:52:30 3/22/96* (0)

Post A Message!

Name:

E-Mail:

Subject:

Figure 4.2
http://www.cadvantage.com/~calrees/wwwboard/index.html

When encountering such a board just click on the information you want to see and it will take you to another link.

Interactive bulletin boards encourage reactions to messages that others have posted. An example of an interactive system is the 1st District Democrats BBS. This system is a good example of an archive of topics others have discussed. It makes it easy for you to join in. To see the full message of a topic, just click on the link.

Harvesting the Internet for Instructional Resources

The next important skill to develop, is searching the Internet effectively to locate information related to your goals and objectives. Appendix 11 provides a basic introduction to the process for locating the resources you need through using different search engines.

You will notice as you work with URLs (Unique Resource Locators, the formal designation for website addresses) that each location is followed by an extension (.com, .edu, .net). These abbreviations, signify the category or domain in which the location resides. The domain extensions and related corresponding category description are summarized as follows:

.com	commercial
.edu	education
.gov	government
.mil	military
.net	network related
.org	organization (nonprofit organization)

Examples of international sites:

.ac.uk	academic, United Kingdom
edu.au	academic, Australia
.nl	Netherlands
.jp	Japan

As you might expect, the type and quality of information varies among the different categories. A few clues may guide you in your search for quality information on the Internet. Domain names with the extension .gov, .edu., and .mil are most likely to have information of a noncommercial nature. Commercial sites can be excellent resource sites, but the information must be scrutinized to determine whether or not the primary focus is informing or selling. Also look at the date the material was last updated to find out if the information is current. I prefer information less than six months old, but do consider material up to two years old. If the information has not been revised at all since it was created, I generally consider it a stale site—though there are significant exceptions to this rule.

SEARCH POINTERS

1. Use more than one search engine to expand your quest for the best of all the available information. Different search engines present information differently. The Excite search engine provides the percentage of relationship the search should (I stress, *should*) relate to your topic. The Magellan search engine ranks each site according to relevancy using 1 to 4 stars. Alta Vista is also very effective.

2. Don't worry about using the right search engine. Just start searching.

3. Keep track of different search engines as they are constantly improving. Hotbot is currently one of my favorite search engines. In 1997, *PC Magazine* voted it "best." You will find Hotbot in small print under a browser's list of search engines. Recently when I was researching for "Internet Growth," I got much better results with Excite. Excite now offers a new feature that divides information into websites and articles.

4. If you live in the United States and are researching U.S. sites, search early in the morning or late at night for the quickest response times.

5. If you get an overwhelming number of hits for a term you've entered, look at at least twenty-five sources and analyse the kind of information the search produced. If the information is irrelevant, experiment with different search terms. Normally review at least fifty sources to locate the best resources. I usually won't give up on a search until I have scanned about one hundred sources. Not all the sources will be active, some will be listed more than once and some will have no apparent relationship to your search—though the computer would not have returned them unless your search term occurred somewhere in the document.

Additional help in learning to search the Internet effectively can be found through Faculty Connection, an Internet site that offers three levels of tutorials—novice, intermediate, and expert—that specifically meet the needs of educators. Its message speaks for itself (http://faculty.creativeanalytics.org/).

Welcome to the Faculty Connection! This website is designed to assist faculty of post-secondary institutions to become familiar with issues, examples and discussion topics associated with using emerging technologies in teaching and learning. Using the website, faculty are encouraged to travel the web at a comfortable pace to identify (a) where courses are offered over the Internet (b) how technology can be used in the classroom, and to discuss (c) strategic issues that will affect them in the future. Please choose your route! (Creative Analytics, Inc., 1997).

Assessment of Websites

The prolixity and variable quality of Internet sites require that we carefully evaluate the sources that we find. As Hope Tillman writes in "Evaluating Quality on the Net": "Within the morass of networked data are both valuable nuggets and an incredible amount of junk" (1997).

The assessment tool, Evaluation for Quality of Web Sites, provides a review of key points to consider (see Appendix 4.2). Because each of us will have different criteria for what constitutes quality, this tool provides a frame of reference to help identify four quality indicators of websites: authority, accuracy, timeliness, and bias.

I start with the basic assumption that information from sites with an education (.edu), government (.gov), or organizational (.org) extension generally have more credibility as a source of quality information. This does not mean that commercial (.com) sites do not provided excellent information—you just need to scrutinize them for intent and bias.

Technical Evaluation of Web Sites (see Appendix 4.3) specifies important technical features of a website such as ease of navigation and speed of downloads. Some sites use too much animation and other glitzy features that can slow down performance and lead to considerable frustration.

Subjective Assessment of Web Sites (see Appendix 4.4) explores more personal responses to sites. Visual or novelty appeal can be qualities you'll sometimes want to use to introduce student Web courses. However, quality must be met first.

The assessment of design based on learning principles is addressed in Chapter 9, Web–related Assessment and Evaluation.

Integrating the Web in Teaching through Self-directed Modules

As already noted, traditional class handouts, course outlines, and PowerPoint presentations all provide potential raw material for Web pages—lecture notes become Internet postings. The next building block for creating Internet-based learning is the conversion of course modules into online learning elements. A sequence of modules can constitute a complete online course.

Since the '70s I have used one or more modules in almost every class to serve as the basic sources of content to supplement mini lectures. In one course, a graduate media class, most of the content is presented via modules, though I still often begin a class with mini lectures. I am now switching from distributing modules in hardcopy in class to providing them online through a Web site. Whatever the form, it's important to comply with copyright laws. In times of tight budgets, converting print materials to Web format saves money. Tests can also be administered online, with the students' grades returned to them immediately.

Maise (1996) points out that the instructional material of tomorrow is going to be assembled —not single authored—from multiple sources of content. For example, most of my self-directed modules include links to related content that I've found on the Internet. Each semester, I do new searches and update the modules.

Once you have developed your first module, you can save it as a template and reuse the basic outline repeatedly with different content. Modules are easy to adapt to different situations. See Chapter 1 for a list of key module elements.

When creating a new module, I begin with my objectives. However, in the process I often find information that challenges to me to rethink my original objectives and perhaps add others.

A completed module is provided for you to adapt as either an online or offline teaching tool. (See Appendix 4.5 for an example of an on-line module).

POINTERS FOR DEVELOPING MODULES

1. Each component of the module is important.

2. As with any content, begin with the objective and then search for information to assemble.

3. Write a paragraph to describe the purpose of the module.

4. Not all modules will have reading assignments; but students will learn to look at this section to check the reading assignments.

5. Omit Web sections if learners do not have access to the technology.

6. Define key terms to help learners focus on important concepts.

7. Developing and using modules is not about technology. Modules help learners take their first self-directed learning steps. They are also an effective way for educators to take their first steps in teaching content without lecturing.

8. It is virtually impossible to identify every step the learner should take in the module. Ambiguity is part of the process and problem solving is part of discovery.

9. Provide a conclusion to measure whether whether objectives have been met. I have just started adding new information to this section: "What's Due" and "When." These two pieces of information were a great hit with students.

By evaluating each module, you can then revise any section that didn't work. It is rare for me to have a perfect module the first time it is developed. I always date each version of the module and improve it each time the module is used.

Some of the most important feedback that I have received has been from the module evaluation tool, which is discussed in the chapter 9. Spontaneous reactions are important to me and I encourage subjective feedback by eliciting responses such as "The thing that I most liked about this module" and "The thing I least liked about the module was . . . " Responses expand to include anything about me or the course that students feel warrants comments. Some recent comments from a graduate public relations class who were just beginning to use modules on the Web include the following:

LIKED

This module was easier to understand—maybe I am getting used to the subject after the previous modules.

Gave an overview of public relations in healthcare and was effective in helping me get the basic ideas.

The book was clear and relevant. Outside articles do help in gaining another perspective.

I learned a lot from the article links. I also copied other Web articles that I thought were interesting.

The thing that I liked most about this module was that it was online and interactive. Very impressive.

Linking to Web sites of interest—most definitely! The text is OK, but to see what is currently online is much better than a book any day.

I liked the introduction to public relations that the module provided. I really like how the module works, it provides an excellent guide for learning.

DISLIKED

Having problems at home while I'm online.

I was a little unclear as to the role that the Web sites played with respect to this module assignment—not because of the relevance of the sites but more because of the new form of self-directed learning.

The Web assignments were a bit confusing.

I kept finding interesting topics and then went off on tangents. (Actually, that's not a bad thing!)

The Web assignments were stressful, time consuming, and unnecessary.

I guess I disliked the detailed information regarding the various types of new methods of public relations research. I realize it is important, but I feel overloaded with detailed information.

The research link didn't work. :-(

Designing and utilizing modules is always a work in progress. Lectures, of course, are also works in progress. However, with modules, you can review each portion separately and continually improve each one: directions, content, and over-all functionality of the learning experiences. Start with one module and then slowly add more, as you become more comfortable with the process.

In the future designing and building modules and online instruction will involve the assembling of information in formats such as sound files, music, animations, Portable Document Format (PDF) files, shocked programs (multimedia extensions for your browser), and video.

Integrating Elements with an Interactive Course Manager

Betty Collis's (1996) interactive integrator (http://utto237.to.utwente.nl/ism/online96/online96/html) inspired my use of a course manager to connect the various features of a course. My course manager has interrelated elements that are represented by icons in a table format. The students interact with the course manager by selecting an icon to take them to the desired feature. The intent of the course manager is to provide a seamless link to important course features.

SUGGESTED FEATURES OF A COURSE MANAGER

- A *news feature* link to provide on-going news related to the course.

- A *module* icon that links to another Web page with a list of all the modules available.

- A *conference* icon to take students straight to the collaborative software you use for your course.

- A *chat room* link to provide a place for students to meet with each other, with other individuals, or with me as desired. Students may need to be reminded that they have to set up a time to meet as no one wants to hang out alone in a chat room.

- *Listserv* links to allow electronic connectivity with others who are not enrolled in the course or who are outside your institute who have a common interest in the topic.

- *Face-to-face* link to remind students to set up appointments for office hours when they need help.

- An *e-mail link* with an automatic mail message pop-up to allow students to quickly write a message without having to look up an e-mail address.

Figure 4.3 shows a completed course manager for a graduate course that only uses a few of these elements. You will have your own ideas of what you will need to build your own course manager.

Figure 4.3 A Completed Course Manager for a Graduate Course

Utilizing Collaborative Conferencing Systems

According to David Wooley: "The field of Web-conferencing software is growing at a breathtaking pace. In the summer of 1994 there were exactly two products in this category, both of them rather primitive freeware packages. Today there are well over 60 commercial and freeware products, many of them quite sophisticated, that support conferencing on the web in one form or another" (1996).

The first challenge faced by educators wanting to use collaborative systems is the selection of an interactive conferencing system. Two are discussed at the end of this chapter. Kindberg (1997) offers the following suggestions for desirable features in a conferencing system.

1. *Managing technical features.* When working with groups, there needs to be a reasonably short time lag between a user-interface action (e.g. clicking on a button) and seeing the results on the screen.

2. *Object control.* Consistency requirements vary between objects, so concurrency control needs to be applied selectively. For example, it may not matter if two views of a shared whiteboard differ by a pixel or two; but it is critical that two views of the same part of a shared document do not differ textually.

3. *Ability to Recover.* The overall effect of changes that several users make concurrently can be hard to predict, so it is essential that users should be able to recover previously agreed versions of shared objects.

4. *Security.* Designated users should be able to apply a security policy such as a password for the protection of objects and privacy of communication .

5. *Limit access.* Another unit of protection is allowing only designated users to use the system.

6. *Importing documents.* Users should be able to import different types of files into the system.

7. *Audio communication.* For some individuals, audio is essential for serious synchronous collaborative work, but because of bandwidth and latency limitations it remains to be seen how successfully networked audio can be integrated (as opposed to using external telephone links).

8. *Use of familiar resources.* There needs to be support for objects that are not part of the system. While providing a framework for objects that may be used by the group as a whole, such as collaborative document editors, the system needs to support objects that can only be created and edited by single users using conventional tools. For example, it should allow an author to create a file in MS-Word and install it into the system for others to view.

While there are now many conferencing systems, only two will be described. Lotus Notes is a commercial system and Germany's Basic Support of Cooperative Work (BSCW) is a free public system.

Lotus Notes is a very good system. Milter and Stinson contend that Lotus Notes " . . . not only enables, but substantially enriches our MBA Program (1995). " They see a collabora-

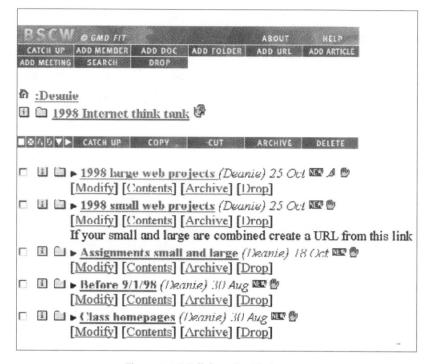

Figure 4.4 A Collaborative Workspace

tive system that " . . . places the learner into exactly the type of projects and work situations that he/she will face as a leader in the information age organizations of the twenty-first century. Specifically students gain these success skills:

1. Learn basic business skills within the context of the work world.

2. Develop basic skills (communication, collaboration and teamwork).

3. Develop personal characteristics (initiative, creativity, personal responsibility).

4. Develop a level of comfort with information technology.

5. Develop computer-driven professional presentations.

The next challenge is to build student interaction and course involvement. Students have to be taught how to establish online interactive communication. It is a vital first step to get everyone successfully signed on the system; and to then to build tasks for collaboration from simple to complex.

The BSCW won first place in the 1996 European Software Innovation Prize (ESIP '96). When I saw Collis's use of this system, I knew it was the missing element I needed to enhance communication between students and students, as well as, teacher and students.

BSCW is a shared workspace, a general tool that can be used, for example, to store documents (or other objects) that relate to some particular project or working group. The important benefits are:

You can use the workspace to share documents across different platforms (Windows, Macintosh, or Unix).

You can access a workspace, browse through folders, and retrieve objects just like ordinary WWW pages.

You can upload documents via a WWW-Browser.

The workspace keeps you aware of all events (e.g., creating, reading, changing of objects)

You do not need to install any software if you use the BSCW-server at GMD – the German National Research Centre for Information Technology. You only need an ordinary Web browser. (But you can install BSCW on your own server if you want, and you may download additional software for uploading to ease the use of the workspace.) (http://bscw.gmd.de/) Figure 4.4, a collaborative workspace illustrates a workspace for a graduate course, HHR 5332.

In conclusion, both teachers and learners have to adapt to new styles of teaching and learning to meet future learning needs. We are limited or exanded by the enviroments in which we teach or work. Novices and experts need to build institutional networking to identify and locate all possible resources and individuals that can share their experiences. It takes proactive movement and a strong desire to move into this dynamic instructional area.

Appendix 4.1: How to Internet

http://attila.stevens-tech.edu/~mlazarev/aka/

BY ROBERT GRODY

(Reprinted by permission of the author. *This has been slightly modified to present as a print resource.*)

Every evening, late, while you are sleeping, robots are roaming the Web. They read and reread Web pages, counting words, letters, recording all that has changed. These automated records are deposited into databases, waiting silently, patiently, to be searched.

Of course, no one robot can search each and every page on the Web. They specialize. Some specialize in being general. Each one has its particular formula. The combinations of which pages a robot chooses to search, how it counts data, and many other factors combine to make each one's results unique. The common name for these robots is *SEARCH ENGINE.*

Search engines are commercial entities, although accessing them is free. They make their money by charging advertisers based on the traffic on each site. To use a search engine, go to its HOME PAGE to enter a set of KEYWORDS on which you would like a report. You may have heard names like Yahoo, Alta Vista, Lycos, Excite. All are Search Engines.

To use INFOSEEK, you must open its HOME PAGE, www.infoseek.com, OR you can click on a browser option, "Internet Search." There you'll find a page with several search engines side by side, allowing you to compare results. A page called Search.com contains over 250 different search engines.

There should be a bright LINK called Tips. Most Search Engines will include such a link; keep an eye open for it. Clicking there will bring a page of rules for getting the best results. INFOSEEK Search Tips (These tips also work with other search engines.)

Click in the search box and type a few words that describe what you want to find. Using English words and phrases, without special symbols or punctuation, works best. However, you can sometimes refine your searches by using special syntax in your search.

FINDING PROPER NAMES

Capitalize proper names, such as "December" and "California. "

If you capitalize adjacent names, Infoseek Guide treats the words as a single name. For example, to find sites that mention actress Rain Phoenix, type: **Rain Phoenix**

If you don't capitalize a proper name, it will be treated like any other word. Typing "rain phoenix" will find sites about weather and Phoenix (AZ), rather than information about River's sister.

If you want to search for several names, use commas to separate the different names. For example, to search for Babe Ruth and the Boston Red Sox, type: **Babe Ruth, Boston Red Sox**

Omitting the comma between proper names causes them to be treated as one single long name. A search for

Babe Ruth Boston Red Sox yields no results.

FINDING A PHRASE

Use double quotation marks around or hyphens between words that are part of a phrase.

Use double quotation marks (" ") around words that must appear next to each other. For example, to find pages that describe stupid pet tricks, type:

"stupid pet tricks"

Without the double quotation marks, Infoseek Guide would find sites that include the word **stupid**, sites that include the word **pet**, and sites that include the word **tricks**. The search results would include information about "stupid Mac tricks," "stupid Internet tricks," and "stupid OS/2 tricks," as well as pages about funny animal antics.

Do not use single quotation marks (' ') in place of double quotation marks.

Use hyphens (-) between words that must appear within one word of each other. For example, to search for information about cable networks, type:

cable-networks

Without the hyphen, Infoseek Guide looks for sites that include the word **cable** and the word **networks**. The search results would include information about setting up Ethernet and token ring computer networks. With the hyphen, Infoseek Guide finds references to radio or television cable networks such as CNN.

FINDING WORDS THAT APPEAR TOGETHER

Use brackets to find words that appear within 100 words of each other, such as words you would expect to see in the same sentence or paragraph. For example, to find safety tips for using elevators, type:

elevator safety

Infoseek Guide finds sites containing safety information for different universities in the United States. With the brackets, it finds the home page for the National Association of Elevator Safety Associates.

SPECIFYING WORDS THAT MUST APPEAR IN THE RESULTS

Put a plus sign (+) in front of words that must be in documents found by the search. For example, to find city guides about San Francisco, type:

city guide +San Francisco

Do not put a space between the plus sign (**+**) and the word.

SPECIFYING WORDS THAT SHOULD NOT APPEAR IN THE RESULTS

Put a minus sign (-) in front of words that should not appear in any documents found by the search. For example, to find all resources that contain python but not monty, type:

python -monty

Do not put a space between the minus sign (-) and the word.

Appedix 4.2 Evaluation for Quality of Web Sites

Different professionals will have different beliefs about what is "quality" information on the Internet. This instrument provides a frame of reference to help identify four quality indicators : *authority, accuracy, timeliness*, and *bias*. Overall, there is a basic assumption that information that comes from an education (.edu), government (.gov), or organizational (.org) source tends to be quality information. There are always exceptions. However, excellent information can come from commercial (.com) sites. Providing needed information is an effective community relations marketing tool. An example of each type of resource information is found in Table 4.1, Source and Type of Information. The selections are arbitrary, since the Internet abounds in examples. The table also provides addresses for the examples.

TABLE **4.1** SOURCE AND TYPE OF INFORMATION		
Address code	**Examples of source**	**Address**
Education (.edu)	SWT Graduate catalog	http://www.gradschool.swt.edu/gradcat.htm
Goverment (.gov)	OSHA Computerized Information System	http://www.osha-slc.gov/
	U.S. Department of Labor, Occupational Safety and Health Administration regulations.	
Organization (.org)	American Society for Training and Development	http://www.astd.org/
	Web site for ASTD, the world's premiere association for training	
Commercial (.com)	Welcome to Microsoft	http://www.microsoft.com/

QUALITY INDICATORS

Four quality indicators provide a framework to assess information found across different types of Web sources (.edu, .gov, .org, .com).

1. **Authority** is the most important criteria. If authority is not clear, the data is highly questionable from the beginning. Indicators of authority include: clear ownership of the page; links to the purpose of the sponsor; and verification information to contact sponsor (ie. name, e-mail address, phone number, or address). The greater the amount of information

about the ownership of the page and the purpose of the site, the greater the likelihood of assessing quality.

2. **Accuracy** is essential. Indicators of accuracy include: sources of information that can be verified by another source, clarity regarding who holds responsibility for the information, and current hyperlinks to other Web pages. Most sites have hyperlinks to other sites and these sites can be verified by the same criteria as the homepage. For example, many sites have hyperlinks that point to other rich sources of information. MedAcess Health Information Resources in the Federal Government is an excellent starting point to provide a strong base for additional research from the hyperlinks. Grammatical, spelling, and HTML errors raise questions about accuracy and possible quality of the information.

3. **Timeliness** is one of the most important features on the Web to respond to fast paced and changing information. Each document should have the date that the document was last revised. In most situations, individuals cannot access older editions. Older versions should not contain better information.

4. **Bias** is one of the confounding factors on the Web. For example, the Southwest Texas graduate catalog is designed to make the Graduate School appear attractive. However this does not detract from the quality of the information. The catalog still meets the criteria of authority, accuracy, and currency. Commercial sites often are trying to sell their services. However, many do provide quality information and can meet three indicators of quality: authority, accuracy, and timeliness.

REFERENCES

Grassing, Esther. 1996. "Thinking Critically about World Wide Web Resources. " (http://www.library.ucla.edu/libraries/college/instruct/critical.htm)

MdLachlan, Karen. 1996. WWW CyberGuide Ratings for Content Evaluation. (http://www.cyber-bee.com/guide1.html).

Tate, Marsha. 1966. "Teaching Critical Evaluation Skills for World Wide Web Resources. " Computers in Libraries, 16, 10, 49–55.

Appendix 4.3 Technical Evaluation of Web Sites

URL of Web Site being evaluated: http:// _____

1. Does the home page download efficiently?   YES/NO
COMMENTS

2. First impression/general appearance
Does the page make a positive first impression?   YES/NO
Does the page have strong eye appeal?   YES/NO
Do you want to explore the site further?   YES/NO
Are the graphics in proportion to the text?   YES/NO
COMMENTS:

3. Ease of navigation
Can you quickly move from page to page?   YES/NO
From link to link?   YES/NO
Are there sufficient links for forward and/or backward movement?   YES/NO
Are there links to helpful sites?   YES/NO
COMMENTS

4. Use of graphics/sound/video
Do the graphics add to the content of the page?   YES/NO
Does the use of sound complement the page?   NA/YES/NO
Does the video make a significant contribution?   NA/YES/NO
COMMENTS

5. Is the content and information clearly labeled and organized?   YES/NO
COMMENTS

6. Is the address of a contact person available?   YES/NO

7. When was the web site last updated?   DATE: _____

Appendix 4.4 Subjective Assessment of Web Sites

Use this form to assist assessing immediate reactions to a site or to make comparisons among two or more Web sites. Enter a check mark or X in any applicable box. Your entries should be made from your first reaction to each site. After you have entered your responses, go back to each site and examine the site slowly and objectively to determine what produced each initial reaction. Use the data you gather doing this review to improve your own Web pages for maximum subjective appeal.

Descriptors	1	2	3	4	5	Comments and Ideas
WOW						
Pretty						
Informative						
Slick						
Fun						
Boring						
Magnificent						
Nice						
Cumbersome						
Organized						
Disorganized						
Messy						
Slow						
Classy						
Colorful						
Terrible						
Interesting						
Busy						
Comments						

References

Allen Communication. 1997. (http://ww4.choice.net/~prosys/software.htm).

Creative Analytics Inc. 1997. "Faculty Connections." (http://faculty.creativeanalytics.org/).

DeMott, Kenneth. 1996. "Evaluation of Computer Assisted Instruction Using Criteria based on Principles of Learning Theory." (http://parsons.ab.umd.edu/~kdemott/ pages/ eval.html).

French, Deanie. 1986. "Using Learning Theory to Design and Evaluate Computer-Assisted Instruction Software." *Nurse Educator* 11 (5), 33–37.

Hickman, Cara. 1995. "Architects, Arhitecture and the Internet." ARCH Research Presentation. November 2, 1997. (http://www.arch.unsw.edu.au/subjects/arch/ resproj/hickman/ netarch.htm).

Kemp, J., Morrison, G., and Ross, S. 1994. *Designing Effective Instruction.* (New York: Macmillan.)

Kindberg, Tim. 1996. "A Framework for Collaboration and Interaction across the Internet." (http://www.dcs.qmw.ac.uk/research/distrib/Mushroom/CSCWWeb.html).

Maise, Elliot. 1996. "The Next Learning Trend: On-The-Fly." *Omega Performance Journal*, Spring 97. (http://shell5.ba.best.com/~jaycross/private/masie.htm)

Maclean, Rodger. 1997. "Notes and Trends." *The Journal of Continuing Higher Education*, Spring 1997, 43.

McClintock, R. and Kim Taipale. 1997. "Computer-mediated Communication." (http://www.ilt.columbia.edu/academic/classes/TU5020/TU5020SY.html).

National Institute of Health. 1995. "Applications, Benefits, and Consequences: The ABCs of Interactive Technology." (http://cgsb.nlm.nih.gov/monograp/tlc/abcs.html).

Nichols, G. 1995. "Formative Evaluation of Web Based Training." (http://www.ucalgary.ca/~gwnichol/formeval/formeval.html).

Tillman, Hope. 1997. "Evaluating Quality on the Net." http://www.tiac.net/users/hope/findqual.html

Treuhaft, J. 1995. "Changes in Education." (http://www.algonquinc.on.ca/edtech/ change.html).

University of Maine (1995). "Definitions for User Interface Rating Tools." http://kramer.ume.maine.edu/cev/defs.html#cog.

"Why should I use BSCW?" http://bscw.gmd.de/Help/sec-11.html

Vogt, E. 1997. "Learning Out of Context." *Omega Performance Journal*, spring (http://shell5.ba.best.com/~jaycross/private/context.htm).

Corporate Background. 1997. "The Webchat Broadcasting System." (http://wbs.net/wbs/press/corporatebackround.html).

Wooley, David. 1996. "Choosing Web Conferencing Software." (http://www.umuc.edu/iuc/cmc96/papers/wool-p.html).

Internet-based Learning Tools

EXAMPLES OF USE FROM INDUSTRY

Dave Harris

The use of Internet-based learning in industry is growing rapidly. This chapter will examine different Internet-based learning tools and look at examples of each. The tools examined here include e-mail, listservs, static Web pages, interactive Web pages, Web based bulletin boards, chat, online courses, and Electronic Performance Support Systems (EPSS). Although the tools will be examined separately, many Internet-based learning scenarios use more than one. As technology changes and we gain more experience, new ways to develop and deliver Internet-based learning will be used.

The purpose of this chapter is to let you explore some examples of what is being done today. This should lead to thoughts of your own about how Internet-based learning could be used in your environment. There is no attempt in this chapter to show the best example for each tool or to show industry best practices. Since your environment is different from mine, we would probably not agree on what is best anyway.

For this chapter, *learning* is defined as gaining new knowledge or new skills, or enhancing current knowledge or current skills. This is a broad stroke approach to defining learning, but Internet-based learning approaches are being used to deliver much more than formal training. *Industry* includes any organization that is not a formal education institution. Industry includes commercial, nonprofit, government, and military organizations.

Sites on the Internet have been chosen to illustrate the examples. Rather than trying to depict the sites with screen captures and words, I have chosen to include the URL and a description of the chosen site. It is recommended that you log on to the Internet and examine the selected sites as you read this chapter. Links to sites as well as links to other sites discovered after this chapter was written can be found on the Harris Training & Consulting Services, Inc. Internet-based Learning Examples page (http://www.htcs.com/ iblex.htm). The sites selected were chosen to illustrate the use of an Internet-based learning mode only. I do not endorse any of the sites selected or guarantee the accuracy of the information found there.

Although examples have been chosen that have a good chance of remaining active, I cannot guarantee that the examples used here will still exist when you read this. So, I have also included applicable search terms for each tool. You can use these terms to perform your own Internet search and find your own examples.

E-mail

E-mail may be the simplest approach to delivering information that can result in learning. E-mail is typically used as a support mechanism for other modes of Internet-based learning or as an asynchronous discussion medium. However, two ways e-mail might be used to promote learning are to deliver one-time procedures and to deliver an ongoing newsletter.

One-time procedures could be delivered by e-mail where e-mail is the easiest form of communication or where the procedure needs to be customized for each recipient. For example, a new employee procedure could be e-mailed to each new employee. Information about benefits, holidays, hours, reporting procedures, and other new employee information could be included in the e-mail and tailored to the new employee's date of hire, position, group, and department.

E-mail can be used to deliver a regular newsletter. In a recent message on the Training and Development List, David Ferguson offered the following suggestions for creating an e-mail based newsletter:

- Concentrate on the content. Write a newsletter your audience wants to read.
- Include an issue identification and headline in the subject. This makes it easy to track back issues.
- Open the newsletter with a description of the contents.

- Make the text easy to read. Use white space, an easy to read font, and headers. Use proper punctuation and spelling.

SquareOne Technology (http://www.squareonetech.com/newsletr.html) offers a free newsletter geared toward Internet use. The August 1997 issue offers "Search Engine Secrets," an article describing how to perform searches on the Web.

Loretta Weiss-Morris is the editor and publisher of the *Quick Training Tips Newsletter*. In this newsletter, you will find "Training Tips, New Requests for Assistance, and Answers to Previous Requests. " This article provides a nice combination of tips from the editor as well as questions and responses by people who receive the newsletter. To subscribe to the *Quick Training Tips Newsletter*, send an e-mail with "subscribe tips" in the subject line to loretta@panix.com.

To find other examples of e-mail delivered information, try searching on "e-mail newsletters. "

Listservs

A listserv is another method for using e-mail to distribute information and to provide asynchronous communication. A listserv is essentially an automated service that forwards messages to everyone on the list. Special software is installed on a server to run a listserv. To join a list, you subscribe to the list. To be removed from a list, you unsubscribe from the list.

Listservs can be one way information distributors or can be discussion lists. A *one way information distribution list* means you receive messages from the list, but cannot post a message on the list. This type of list is used to provide information to members of an organization or to a specific group of people. If you subscribe to a *discussion list*, you and all of the other members will be able to post messages to the list. This means you can ask questions, post responses, and otherwise carry on asynchronous discussions.

Once you subscribe to a list, you will begin receiving messages from the list owner and other members of the list. The messages will be sent to your e-mail address. Through the digest option, you can select to get just one message a day that is a collection of all of the messages sent that day. This is called a *digest*. Or, you can select to receive the messages as individual e-mail messages.

To reply to a message or ask a question, you send a message to the list. Your message is then received by everyone on the list.

Listservs can be set up for a general purpose or for a specific purpose. The listserv may be in existence for a short period of time or forever, depending on its purpose. For example, if you are a member of a collaborative project, you may want to set up a listserv to facilitate communication among the project team members. This listserv would only need to exist for the life of the project. On the other hand, if you want to start a list for training and development professionals around the world, you could anticipate running this list for a very long time.

Listservs can be moderated or unmoderated. A *moderated list* means the listserv manager reviews each message before it is posted to the list. The result is messages that are not relevant, contain personal attacks or flames, or are inappropriate, never get posted to the list.

TRDEV-L LISTSERV

TRDEV-L is a listserv discussion group for training and development. In fact, it is one of the most popular listservs on the Internet. This listserv now has over five thousand subscribers from at least sixty different countries. As with any group this size, the conversations are varied and wide ranging. Although the listserv is sponsored by Penn State's Center for Academic Computing and the Workforce Education and Development Program in Penn State's College of Education, the subscribers on the list have all types of training and development backgrounds and come from many industries. If you are involved in training and development, you will want to at least try this listserv. More information and subscribing instructions can be found at http://train.ed.psu.edu/trdev-l/ welcome.html.

CHANGE LISTSERV

If you are interested in implementing change in your organization, you might want to try the CHANGE listserv. This list is for anyone in industry or education who wants to explore initiating and sustaining change. To subscribe to this list, send an e-mail to MAJOR-DOMO@MINDSPRING.COM. In the text of the message, write subscribe CHANGE.

SUBSCRIPTION TOOLS

There are thousands of listservs you can subscribe to. Fortunately, there are several tools that you can use to find a listserv that you may be interested in. Two of the tools are Tile.Net Lists and the List of Lists.

Tile.Net Lists (http://www.tile.net/tile/listserv/index.html) lets you view a list of list-servs by description, name, subject, host country, and sponsoring organization. In addition, you can perform searches to zero in on a particular topic of interest.

With the List of Lists (http://catalog.com/vivian/interest-group-search.html) you can search one of the largest databases of listservs on the Internet. The results of the search include the list name, a description of the list, the subscription address, and the list owner. This site also includes other information about lists and listservs.

If you still want more information on listservs, try searching on **listservs**. A recent search using Hotbot (http://www.hotbot.com/) resulted in over 7000 matches for the search term **listservs**. To refine the search, try searching on listservs plus a topic of interest. A search on **listservs training** resulted in 1678 matches.

Static Web Pages

Static Web pages are a method used to present information. The purpose of a static Web page is to impart information to the reader. The term *static* refers to the fact that this is a one-way mode. The reader reads the page and does not interact with the page itself. A static Web page does not have to be boring. Any possible Web technique can be used on a static Web page including text, graphics, sound, and video.

Static Web pages may contain information that is stable or it may contain information that changes frequently. In either case, by definition, static Web pages are a one-way mode. Static Web pages may include journal articles, white papers, procedures, policies, presentations, and any other information the Web page publisher wants to impart to the reader.

As was mentioned in the Introduction, more than one tool is often used. Web pages are often accompanied by the use of e-mail, Web-based bulletin boards, or chats to provide interaction in a scenario where static Web pages are providing the information.

The *Intranet Journal* (http://www.intranetjournal.com/) offers a wide variety of information about Intranets and Extranets. Articles, Frequently Asked Questions (FAQs), and opinion pieces are among the information offered on this site.

Creating a Knowledge Centric Information Technology Environment is a paper I wrote and published on the Web. The paper is available at http://www.htcs.com/ckc.htm. This is an example of a static Web page. It is intended to be read as any printed or online paper would be read.

John S. Denker has produced an online book called *See How It Flies* (http://www. monmouth.com/~jsd/how/title.html). This book includes flight procedures for pilots.

The Office of Technology Policy (OTP) (http://www.ta.doc.gov/OTPolicy/default.htm) is a federal government office that develops and advocates national policies on the use of technology to build America's economic strength. This site includes programs, services, speeches, and publications from the OTP.

An example of a presentation available on the Internet is "Internet Trends and Technologies Briefings: Internet Search Engines," a presentation made by Greg R. Notess at the Online World Conference 1996. This presentation is available at http://www.imt. net/~notess/speak/ol96/index.html.

Since static Web pages make up most of the World Wide Web, numerous examples can be found on any topic. To find other examples, search on the topic you are interested in.

Interactive Web Pages

Many Internet sites, including commercial sites, are using interactive Web pages to offer you more from the site. Interactive Web pages include the ability to search a database, ask questions, customize the look and feel of the site, sing along, and perform other types of interactivity. For our purposes, online courses are not included here. They are addressed elsewhere.

Interactive Web pages are the next evolution in Web page design. You will find many examples as you explore the Internet.

You can analyze a Web page or an entire Web site by using the tools available at Doctor HTML (http://www2.imagiware.com/RxHTML/). This Interactive Web site will help you create good Web pages by testing your pages for you.

The *Wall Street Journal* Interactive Edition (http://www.wsj.com/) offers twenty-four-hour news, a personal-financial service, a searchable news archive, and the ability to easily navigate through the news you are interested in. This is a subscription site, and a good example of what can be done with interactive Web pages.

A test for fun can be found at the BrainTainment Center (http://www.brain.com/welcome.html). In addition to information about brainpower, you are offered a free online

IQ test. This is a commercial site and you are encouraged to buy products. However, it contains a good example of an online interactive test.

At the School House Rock site (http://www.schoolhouserock.com/index-l.html), you can download the School House Rock songs, read the words online, and sing along.

Although not nearly as common yet as static Web pages, the number of sites deploying interactive Web pages continues to grow. To find other examples, search on the topic you are interested in or try combining your topic with any of the following terms: **interactive**, **explore**, **online**, or **search**.

Web-based Bulletin Boards

Web-based bulletin boards allow an ongoing asynchronous conversation. Bulletin boards are text based, but usually allow links to URLs. This allows you to direct the reader to a Web page you may be discussing, or that contains more information. Bulletin boards can be used to support conversations on any topic. Like listservs, bulletin boards may be set up for a general purpose or a specific purpose. And, like listservs, bulletin boards may have a short lifetime or a very long lifetime. Bulletin boards can be a good learning medium for collaborative projects, discussions on general topics, and supporting more formal courses. Bulletin boards are often used in conjunction with other modes to create a complete learning scenario.

The TrainingSuperSite offers a Web-based bulletin board (http://www.trainingsuper-site.com/TSS_Link/DisBoardSet.htm) as a medium for discussing training issues. This bulletin board is open to anyone who is interested in training.

The American Immigration and Citizenship Center has a Web-based bulletin board (http://us-immigration.iserver.com/newsgroup_dir/guestlg.html) where questions about immigration are answered.

The National Federation of Independent Business (NFIB) Online (http://www.nfibon-line.com/forums/) has several online forums (bulletin boards) related to owning and operating small businesses.

Time Warner's Pathfinder Network has a list of bulletin boards that can be sorted by host or by category. To get to the list of bulletin boards, go to the welcome page (http://www.pathfinder.com) and click on Bulletin Boards.

As you can see from these examples, many bulletin boards exist on the Internet covering a wide range of topics. To find other examples, search on **bulletin boards** or **forums**. To find bulletin board software you can use to set up your own bulletin board, search on **bulletin board software**. To find a bulletin board hosting site, search on **bulletin board host**.

Chat

Chat refers to software that allows participants in a chat "room" to communicate in real time. The majority of chats are still text based with participants typing their messages. Some chat facilities now support audio and video. Chats may be accessible to everyone as in *Internet Relay Chat (IRC)* or may be offered through a service that limits participation to members. Microsoft Network (MSN), Compuserve, and America Online (AOL) all offer a chat or chat-like feature.

Because chat is a real-time communication, it is usually only one tool used in Internet-based learning. Good design of Internet-based learning would include some facility for asynchronous communication. When you implement your own chats, you may want to use IRC or you may want to use one of the chat servers that are coming on the market.

Time Warner's Pathfinder Network has chat rooms where you can participate. Topics include finances and current events. To get to the list of chats, go to the welcome page (http://www.pathfinder.com) and click on **Chat**.

Quarterdeck has chat client and server software available. As a service to the Internet community, Quarterdeck also maintains an Internet Chat Guide (http://www.qdeck.com/qdeck/products/globalchat/schedule.html). The Guide includes links to chats in progress and information about upcoming chats.

Chats on the Internet are very prevalent. You should be able to find a chat on any topic you are interested in. To find chats search on your topic and **chat**. Or, try finding a chat by searching the indexes on Yahoo (http://www.yahoo.com/Computers_and_Internet/ Internet/Chat/Indices/).

Online Courses

Online courses are another growing area of the Internet. Many educational institutions offer online courses as part of their educational programs. Other organizations are also offering online courses. As might be expected, many of the courses are related to using the Internet, developing for the Internet, and other technical topics. However, online courses can be found on many topics. If you are going to develop online courses, I suggest you spend some time on the Internet looking at what other people are doing.

Hart Crowser hosts the Online Institute (http://www.supportonline.com). There is a demonstration course as well as courses that can be taken for a fee. Hart Crowser will also develop and host courses for your company on their site.

ZDNet University (ZDU) also offers online courses. The courses are Internet and technology related. You can access ZDU at http://www.zdu.com/.

Hardwick Publications, Inc. offers online continuing education credit courses for CPAs. The course list and information can be accessed at http://www.bestcpe.com/courses.htm.

Safety Insights offers online safety and health training (http://www.safetyinsights. com/). As of this writing, the first course is free.

The above are just a small sample of the online courses available on the Internet. To find more courses, search on **online courses**. Or, search on the topic you are interested in.

EPSS

An *Electronic Performance Support System (EPSS)* is a computer-based system that receives, stores, and disseminates organizational knowledge and information on demand. An EPSS can be used as part of an Internet-based learning strategy to bring information and training to an employee on demand. The information or training would be directly related to the employee's performance or responsibilities, providing just-in-time assistance to the employee.

Each EPSS is different. They run the gamut from simple stand-alone procedures to complex systems that are knowledge based.

The U.S. Army has developed an EPSS called the Knowledge Worker System. A description and details about this system are available at http://www.cecer.army. mil/kws/.

The EPSS InfoSite contains links to many online examples of browser-based Electronic Performance Support Systems. The links can be found at http://www.tgx.com/enhance/ dddemos.htm.

The Knowledge Connection Corporation has created a report titled *Technology and*

Learning: Innovative Projects In 1996. The report includes several descriptions of innovative EPSS's. The descriptions are available at http://www.tgx.com/enhance/dddemos.htm.

To find more examples of EPSS's on the Internet, search on **EPSS** or **Electronic Performance Support System**.

Conclusion

We have looked at different modes of Internet-based learning. The tools examined here include e-mail, listservs, static Web pages, interactive Web pages, Web-based bulletin boards, chat, online courses, and Electronic Performance Support Systems (EPSS). Although they were examined separately, they can be used together. These examples may help you think about how Internet-based learning could be used in your environment.

Internet-based Learning

WHAT'S IN IT FOR THE ADULT LEARNER?

Barbara Lyman

Internet-based education and training offer many potential benefits specific to adult learners. Currently, the most common theme of adult learning theory is that to be effective, teaching must be learner centered and self-directed (see chapter 1 for a discussion of the Internet and self-directed learning). Those who design and guide Internet-based learning experiences of adults need to consider the full implications of learner-centered instruction. One approach to understanding the adult learner from a holistic perspective is the Model of Situated Learning: Interactivity Among Clusters. This chapter focuses on the implications of the model for Internet-based learning. This model incorporates four factors that affect every learning situation with the learner as central. It also echoes the emphasis of contemporary educational psychology on the individual and the social construction of knowledge, that is, the constructivist perspective on learning (Prawat and Floden 1994; Resnick 1991; Wertsch 1991).

The Model of Situated Learning: Interactivity Among Clusters

The Model of Situated Learning provides a vehicle for looking at major factors critical to design and delivery if we are going to be successful in providing Internet-based learning experiences to adults. The model posits four clusters of factors that affect and mutually influence each other in every learning situation (see figure 6.1). Thus a strength of the model is its emphasis on interactivity among factors. The four mutually influencing clusters of factors in this model include (1) characteristics of the learner, (2) learning goals, (3) the nature of the media for learning, and (4) available learning skills and strategies.

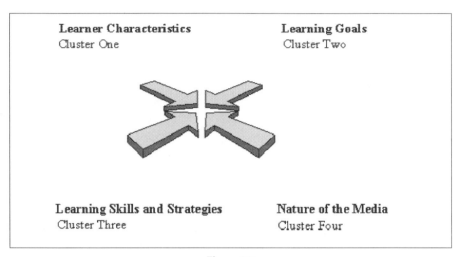

Figure 6.1

A primary advantage of using this model is that it forces us to examine Internet-based learning in a more complete context than we might otherwise. Because the adult learner is central to the discussion of benefits of Internet-based learning, we'll begin by explaining the characteristics of the adult learner. The discussion will proceed to look at other major factors: learning goals, strategies, media, and their interplay in the context of Internet-based learning.

As the discussion proceeds, we will examine benefits of Internet-based learning within the framework of the Situated Learning model. Using the model makes it impossible to talk about the benefits of Internet-based learning in isolation. Thus the use of the word *situated* to refer to the model. The more carefully we think about its major implications in light of factors that impinge on the use of Internet-based learning, the more likely we are to experience enduring success with online learning. To consider the benefits of Internet-based learning for the adult, it is important to begin gaining a better understanding of this audience.

My Personal Illustration
of the Model of Situated Learning

Because this chapter takes a broad view about adults as a general class of learner, it may be helpful to illustrate the Model of Situated Learning more concretely by applying the model to my own adventure in learning Internet-based options for teaching. In review, the four factors posited by the model as important to consider in order to attain effective learning include (a) characteristics of the learner, (b) learning goals; (c) nature of the media for learning; and (d) available learning strategies.

CHARACTERISTICS OF THE LEARNER

Let us consider my characteristics as a learner about the Internet. I am enthusiastic about learning about and from the Internet. As a teacher for a good number of years, I am energized, sensing that I will grow personally and professionally by becoming a proficient user of the Internet. I have not had to be dragged, doing the proverbial kicking and screaming, to the Internet. As many academics are, I am fairly self-directed. Thus I have lots of ideas about what I want from the Internet and why. This gives me a certain focus that I know stands me in good stead in a medium which by its very nature has an embarrassment of riches.

As a learner I have a fairly high tolerance for ambiguity. I do not have to be linear in my development of Internet proficiency. It is fine to gain familiarity in bits and pieces as the multiplicity of other commitments allows time. It is just as acceptable that I do not have all the answers about where the Internet is taking me as a learner who is also a teacher. Part of the excitement is not having all the answers neatly lined up in advance of taking action. I am a ready, willing, and able learner.

LEARNING GOALS

In terms of learning goals, I want to know product and process. I want to know what the capabilities of the Internet are for my purposes and I want to know what to do procedurally to take advantage of the Internet's offerings. It boils down to knowing what (declarative), how (procedural), when, and why using the Internet offers an advantage over other media for reaching my learning goals.

NATURE OF THE MEDIA FOR LEARNING

As a teacher, one of my main learning goals for the Internet is augmenting course content and teaching strategies. I also want to become an even more active online contributor, through course and program websites, e-mail, discussion groups, and collaborative workspaces. For two of the courses I teach, listservs have been set up, and for one of the courses a website has been developed and continues to be revised. The Internet is breathing new life into my professional development. One of the greatest advantages is that I can participate as my schedule permits, from office or from home, and while on the road.

The Internet itself as the medium for learning also impacts the learning situation. The Internet's archival capacity, its multimedia capabilities, and its ability to support interaction among users are prominent features of the medium that affect learning. That the Internet as a medium is still evolving also has implications for learning situations. As vast as the Internet already is, the average user like me can add still more to its databases and home pages, linking these to chains of related sites. The Internet will only grow in terms of the data to which it links me. Its multimedia capabilities will only become more sophisticated yet user friendly and its support for me to work collaboratively with others in asynchronous and synchronous modes is getting better all the time. Getting to the best information in the shortest amount of time will continue to pose challenges within this medium. Efficiency of search engines, the ability to bypass sites that are irrelevant for my purposes, avoiding information put out by unreliable sources, are just a few important considerations in terms of the nature of the Internet medium, this unwieldy venue of free speech and information exchange.

AVAILABLE LEARNING STRATEGIES

The Internet, while it offers so much, requires a great deal of me as a user if I am to be efficient and effective. Therefore, I need the best possible learning strategies. I need metacognitive awareness and control. That is, I need to know myself as a learner, including knowing how I learn best, and monitoring when I am reaching my learning goals and when I am not, i.e., the awareness aspect. If I find that I am not reaching my learning goals, then I need to know what to do to get back on track, i.e., the control aspect. For example, I love to learn. Trivia on a range of subjects is sometimes of inordinate or at least passing interest. Being interested in lots of topics and ideas can be a bit of an affliction when it comes to the Internet. Thus, I realize, because I am metacognitively aware, that I need to know what I want from the Internet during a given search session, be fairly decisive about locating it, eliciting what I need when I find it in the form that I need, and moving on. Without the strategy of self-monitoring or vigilance, then the Internet is subject to make me not more, but less productive and effective as a learner.

I also know I learn best when someone shows me, when I ask "stupid questions," and when I have some time to fiddle around, engaging in trial and error. As long as someone who can help me troubleshoot is within actual or virtual reach I will be more successful than if I engage in lonerism, trying to figure it all out by myself. I know how to take advantage of the intelligence distributed in the environment around me; an important strategy for Internet-based learning. In other words, collaboration is an essential learning strategy. Fortunately, the Internet is equipped in increasingly sophisticated ways to support cooperative learning.

INTEGRATION AND OVERLAP

As is obvious from the illustrations above, the categories of the Model of Situated Learning overlap. That they are not neatly separable does not make them any less useful. Consideration of these factors is critical for developing successful Internet-based learning experiences.

CHALLENGES YOU WILL FACE

What are the characteristics of the learners for whom you would design Internet-based learning?

How can you learn these and take them into account in the design of Internet-based learning experiences?

What are the learning goals of participants?

Are these goals those of the designer of Internet-based instructions? Are the goals appropriate and compatible?

What about the impact of the medium itself on learning? Are you building learning situations that take advantage of the most prominent features of Internet-based learning, i.e., archival capacity, support for interaction, medium for publication, etc., and are you helping learners develop appropriate learning strategies, taking into account learner characteristics, learning goals and expectations, and the nature of the medium itself?

These are just some useful kind of questions to ask as we develop Internet-based learning experiences in our course and training programs. Though there are many questions that can be asked, the Model of Situated Learning serves as a vehicle for reminding us of several of the considerations most important to the success of our efforts.

Cluster 1: Characteristics of Adult Learners

Who are adult learners? What are their characteristics as learners? Which have the greatest implications for the use of Internet-based training whether in industry or educational settings?

Large numbers of adults seek educational experiences. While they do so for a variety of reasons, certain motivations stand out. However, many adults who would benefit greatly from educational experiences fail to seek them out or to persist once underway. The types of barriers that keep adults from participating in education must be addressed adequately if Internet-based learning is to be more successful than traditional media for learning.

According to the U.S. National Household Education Survey (NCES, 1995), 40 percent or 76 million adults took part in adult education during the year preceding the survey. Adult education was defined as participation in systematic learning activities for the purpose of acquiring new knowledge or skills or changing attitudes or values, by persons who have assumed adult social roles (Darkenwald and Merriam as cited in NCES, 1995). The National Household Education Survey excluded traditional college and university education, considering study at such institutions only when it was for the purpose of obtaining licensure or certification for specific occupational fields.

However, large numbers of adults pursue learning in higher education settings. Recent statistics (Tucker 1996) reveal the magnitude of full and part-time participation in higher education in America. An estimated 5.3 million nontraditional undergraduates twenty-five years of age and above are seeking their first degrees. Another 880,000 graduate students twenty-five years of age or older are working towards master's or doctoral degrees. Forecasts indicate that these adult learners, now 44 percent of higher education's student population, will make up over half the higher education student population by the twenty-first century.

REASONS FOR PARTICIPATING IN ADULT EDUCATION

Reasons why adults pursue learning (outside of traditional higher education) have remained fairly consistent over recent decades. The top two reasons have been and continue to be developing work related knowledge and skills and gaining personal development and fulfillment. Recent surveys (NCES 1995) showed that about 20 percent of adults participating in adult education took work-related courses. These included such activities as employer-provided courses, job-related training from other providers, and licensure or certification courses. Similarly, 20 percent of adults participated in personal development learning activities, such as classes related to wellness, hobbies, and Bible study.

The latter types of classes reflect the noncompulsory or postcompulsory nature of much of adult education whereby millions of adults pursue their interests through learning activities on a voluntary basis. Other types of adult education activities in which adults participated, although in much smaller proportions, included 6 percent in credential programs and 1 percent each in apprenticeships, English as a Second Language, and Adult Basic/Adult Secondary Education (NCES 1995).

In accord with the findings of this NCE Survey, earlier surveys of participation in learning adults also cited job-related goals as the number one reason for participating in education activities with personal/social development as a close second (Merriam and Caffarella 1991).

In terms of work related adult education activities, Eurich (1990) delineates three types of need for adults' work-related learning. She states that among technical workers, the trend is toward multiple skills, including teamwork, problem-solving, and technological literacy. For managers, the need to obtain leadership and technical skills, and strategies necessary for the changing world of global competition, continually intensifies. Finally, Eurich cites the need for professionals to update knowledge and skill in their fields as a major reason for continuing education for these adults.

Debates continue about the relative extent to which colleges, universities, corporations, and professional education firms will provide continuing and higher education to adults (Maule 1997; Terhanian 1996; Tucker 1996). At the time of writing it was estimated that in 1997, between $65 and $85 million would be spent by employers on training for adults in the workforce, half of the expenditures going to professional education firms (Tucker 1996). However, regardless of the providers, the use of the Internet by adults continues to

rise quickly. Recent estimates show that of individuals sixteen years of age and older in the United States and Canada, 23 percent are using the Internet and 17 percent are using the Web (CommerceNet/Neilsen Survey 1997; http://www.nielsenmedia.com/).

WHY ADULTS DO NOT PARTICIPATE IN ADULT EDUCATION

While many adults participate in adult education activities, clearly the majority of adults do not. Even the vast majority of adults whose literacy skills are so low as to impede their ability to function in society do not take part in adult education (Kirsch et al. 1993).

Studies have identified a wide range of reasons why adults do not take advantage of educational opportunities. The two most often cited reasons for not participating are *time* and *cost* (Merriam and Caffarella 1991). These and additional deterrents to participation have been categorized in various ways. However, major reasons tend to cluster around *situational barriers* having to do with individuals' life circumstances, *institutional barriers* that include regulatory and procedural impediments to adults accessing educational activities and *dispositional barriers* consisting of adults' beliefs, attitudes, and values (Cross 1981 as cited in Merriam and Caffarella 1991).

Briefly stated, situational barriers to the pursuit of learning and training by adults include the two most frequently implicated obstacles of time and money. Related barriers of this type include lack of adequate transportation and, for parents, lack of appropriate childcare. Lack of family support for adult education endeavors can also impede learners in seeking or completing them (Cams et al. 1995). Often such support is lacking in part because family members have little or no opportunity to become acquainted with the educational activities in which adults are engaged. As will be discussed more fully in succeeding sections and as can be seen in related chapters, Internet-based learning has tremendous potential for saving time and money as well as alleviating related problems of transportation, childcare, and lack of family support.

Institutional barriers to adult participation in learning include any impediments in educational settings and their processes. Noncustomer friendly features that may be part of registering for classes are one example. For instance, processes which allow students to register for courses, while they may actually be unavailable because they are filled or have been cancelled, wastes students time. Some institutions offer online information about course availability that students may consult before registering for such classes or sections. Certainly the Internet has the potential through such database access to cut down on frustrating and time-wasting procedures for learners. Such considerations merit the review of Internet-based educational providers whether in business or higher education.

Dispositional barriers to adult participation in learning activities consist of internal or interacting obstacles having to do with adults' views towards self and learning (Cross 1981 as cited in Merriam and Caffarella). Ranking high among dispositional factors that deter adults from participating in learning programs and courses are attitudes towards self and learning, such as low perception of need, lack of confidence, low personal priority, lack of interest in available courses or programs, lack of awareness of available educational opportunities, and negative attitudes towards education expressed by such statements as "not liking school." Many adults are ashamed of their need for further education, particularly when they require Adult Basic or Secondary Education or any training that could be construed as remedial. This is why adults so often state that they value privacy in learning situations that computer-based instruction may afford (Askov 1994). Dispositional barriers to participation in education by adults merit careful consideration so that Internet-based instruction can be designed and carried out effectively.

GENERAL CHARACTERISTICS OF ADULTS AS LEARNERS

Adult learners are nothing if not diverse. Knowles (1984) characterizes adult learners as:

- Self-directing
- Bringing extensive life experiences on which to build
- Approach learning out of a desire to solve a problem in daily life
- Internally or intrinsically motivated
- Having past learning experiences that may have been negative

Although some adults may bring with them past learning experiences that were negative, in general these negatives are far outpaced by the strengths adults bring to their learning activities. Adults are often so highly motivated that they may be characterized as self-directed learners (see the chapter on self-directed learning for a more complete discussion of this concept) clear in the educational goals and objectives they wish to pursue. This focus may be a particularly valuable characteristic considering the nature of the Internet, as will be discussed further in the next section. The often extensive prior knowledge—and indeed expertise in given areas—that adults bring to the learning experience are of critical importance to new knowledge and skill building. As Ausubel (1963) maintained and subsequent research has strongly supported (see Anderson 1995), the most important factor in what one learns is often what one already knows. Traditional lectures or didactic teaching approaches often fail to capitalize on this rich resource represented by individual and collective prior knowledge of adults. Internet-based learning, if it is based on interactive approaches to learning in which students are treated as co-discoverers of knowledge and asked to work in teams, has the potential to capitalize on adult learners' prior knowledge and experiences in a way that traditional approaches have often failed to do.

Adults are also diverse in their learning styles, having different preferences in terms of the means and media via which they learn. To avoid oversimplifying, learning styles may be most accurately described as sets of conditions under which learners prefer to work. For example, some learners may prefer and learn most readily when information is presented verbally, via print rather than orally, or vice versa. Others may prefer spatial rather than verbal representations, favoring visual organizers such as matrices and network diagrams. Most educators who discuss learning styles promote attempts to teach to various learning styles, while others (Brookfield 1990) argue for teaching both to and against learning preferences so that learners can become more versatile participants in their education. It is probably safe to say that when confronted with difficult concepts and procedures to learn, most learners welcome a variety of presentations and manipulations of the material with which to work. Learners confronted by challenging tasks typically welcome redundancy of information within multiple forms. The multimedia capabilities of the Internet and the Web in particular mean that learners can access on their desktops or portable computers, a variety of means of representation of information as well as opportunities to engage in active learning, working both alone and in concert with others.

To summarize, consideration of the first cluster presented of factors in the Model of Situated Learning reveals that while many adults pursue continuing education, many who would appear to benefit greatly do not. Adults desire to advance their knowledge and skills primarily for work and for personal growth. Adults bring multiple levels and configurations of prior educational attainment and prior knowledge and skills to their educational endeavors. Greater educational opportunities tend to be sought by and provided to those with the highest education levels. Those who fail to pursue further education typically cite time and money as their greatest obstacles. Previous negative educational experiences also play a role. Internet-based learning has the potential to provide the educational development that adult learners need in ways that are appropriate to their needs and backgrounds.

However, as the Model of Situated Learning suggests, learners cannot be considered in isolation from their learning goals, the media for learning, and appropriate learning strategies and skills. In the next section, the factor of learning goals is more fully considered.

Cluster 2: The Learning Goals of Adults

Houle (as cited by Merriam and Caffarella 1991) found that adults taking part in continuing education have three types of goals: (1) *goal-oriented*, education sought in service of achieving some other goal; (2) *activity-oriented*, seeking adult education because of the opportunity to be engaged in the activity itself and to interact socially; and (3) *learning-oriented*, or seeking knowledge for its own sake. The two kinds of goal-oriented educational activities adults seek out most are work-related and personal-development related. Knowles (1984) found that adults approached learning with the goal of solving a problem in daily life. More specific kinds of learning goals emerge in specific contexts.

However, what is perhaps most salient to consider in terms of the learning goals of adults, is that with mature learners, the goals of learning should be open to some negotiation. To the extent that the learning needs of adults differ, based on the different degrees of prior knowledge and experience as well as motivations they bring to learning situations, then trainers and other educators need to respect these differences and take them into account in the design and delivery of instruction. The Internet offers advantages for tailoring instruction to the needs of particular individuals and groups, a topic to which we will turn in the next section.

While the learning goals of adults are a central consideration for those who design Internet-based learning, learning goals defined by other stakeholders must also receive attention. First, while learners' goals must be respected, it is also true that many adults, particularly those who have a history of negative experiences in education, often have internalized dysfunctional concepts of the nature of effective teaching and learning. Students who have struggled mightily under teaching paradigms based on passive learning, such as lecture-only, workbook, or electronic drill-only approaches, often seem to beg for more of the same. In such cases the instructor must gradually win the confidence of students in alternate approaches to learning such as discussion and collaborative learning projects. The Internet provides an opportunity for teachers and learners to break from exclusive use of limited paradigms for teaching and learning.

Learning goals have also been articulated by other stakeholders. For example, two important studies have provided taxonomies of the skills desired by employers. These include the *SCANS* report (1992) and the earlier commission report, *Workplace Basics: The Skills Employers Want* (Carnevale, Gainer, and Meltzer 1990). As a careful look at these reports will show, the skills they describe cumulatively represent many of the marks of the well educated as defined by higher education and by the communities in which we live. The SCANS report highlights, among other sets of foundation skills, thinking skills, including the ability to

- learn
- reason
- think creatively
- make effective decisions and
- solve problems.

Among desired workplace competencies identified by SCANS are the interpersonal skills involving the ability to

- work in teams
- teach others
- serve customers
- lead
- negotiate and
- work well with people form culturally diverse backgrounds

The Carnevale et al. report identifies similar sets of skills classified under the following categories:

1. Organizational Effectiveness/Leadership
2. Interpersonal/Negotiation/Teamwork
3. Self-Image/Goal-Setting-Motivation/Career Development

4.   Creative Thinking/Problem Solving or Resourcefulness

5.   Listening/Oral Communication

6.   Three R's—Reading/Writing/Computation

7.   Learning-to-Learn

The learning goals articulated by all stakeholders in adult education merit considera-tion. The goals of the different stakeholders may often but do not always overlap. What learners want, what higher education defines, and what employers desire all can influence learning situations. The learning goals cluster of the Model of Situated Learning reminds designers of Internet-based learning to consider the voices of various stakeholders as they plan educational experiences.

The breadth alone of the strategies, skills, and knowledge represented by the tax-onomies of the abilities which employers want suggests that learning is a lifelong process. The most widely recognized obstacles to further education that adults typically face are time and money related. Internet-based learning has the potential to deliver a vast array of educational experiences in multimedia and interactively in cost-effective and time-efficient ways. We will more carefully consider the implications of the Internet as a learning medi-um in the next section.

Cluster 3: Learning Media

The Internet's advantages as a learning medium for adults is considerable. Internet-based learning has been described as being able to take "training-enhanced by other media such as videos, animation, and audio—to a widely dispersed audience, *on demand* [empha-sis added]" (Munger 1997, p. 47), with courses or portions of courses available by e-mail, asynchronous conferencing, and real-time conferencing. Entire courses can be down-loaded from the Internet (see the World Lecture Hall home page of the University of Texas at Austin http://www.utexas.edu/world/lecture).

These sites range from simple to elaborate depending on the extent of multimedia used. Martin (1997) has identified five different types of Internet sites available to support adult learning:

- Databases including online libraries and virtual museums

- Learning communities, e.g., listservs and collaborative projects

- Classes and tutorials

- Games and simulations

- Multipurpose learning centers

Examples from different disciplines are found in chapter 3.

As suggested earlier, among the greatest advantages of the Internet is its capacity to address the barriers to education typically faced by adults.

SITUATIONAL BARRIERS AND INTERNET-BASED LEARNING

Understanding how Internet-based learning can remove or at least reduce obstacles adults face in undertaking educational activities calls for a closer look at the three types of barriers adults face in their efforts to pursue further education. The top two situational barriers are time and money. Related situational barriers include lack of adequate transportation and, for parents, lack of appropriate childcare services. Lack of family support for adult education endeavors of learners can also serve as an obstacle (Cams et al. 1995).

In terms of time as a situational barrier, much of adulthood is characterized by taking on multiple roles, each with its own demands of time and, not incidentally, energy. Demands on time arising from multiple roles can obviously all too easily compete with time needed for educational pursuits. Further, time constraints are exacerbated when the schedules for educational courses and programs are incompatible with the work or family schedules of adults. The time it can take to travel to campuses or training sites, that is, location problems, can also impede participation in learning activities. Costs can include obvious barriers, such as tuition and materials fees, that some cannot afford, lost work time, and paying for transportation and child care necessary in order to pursue education.

Many of the time and cost savings associated with Internet-based learning have to do with the three major functions of the Internet identified by Quinlan (1997): *communication* (predominantly the use of e-mail, still the most frequently used tool on the Internet [Starr and Milheim 1996]), *information access* (the Internet's tremendous archival capacity [Shotsberger 1996] from Internet databases to home pages), and *resource sharing* ("the ability to share and publish resources for others to access and use" (Quinlan 1997, p.16). The ease of distributing materials for education and training programs when a "server provides instant distribution to an unlimited number of trainees" (Kruse 1997, p. 60) translates into a cost savings that can be passed on directly to adult learners.

However, the Internet while alleviating some adult education participation barriers associated with time and cost, may contribute to others. For instance, computers and modems are costly. Some adults cannot afford to have Internet access at home. Many workplaces, small businesses in particular, do not provide the kind of computer access that would allow working adults to obtain work-related education and training via the Internet. When adults do have access to computers and modems, these may not always have adequate power or appropriate software to access the multimedia and interactive capabilities that will increasingly characterize Web-based learning.

Even when learners have adequate hardware, features inherent in the Internet may end up wasting the time of adult students. The two most frequently reported problems in a recent survey of Internet users were time (and methods) for finding information, especially as the Web grows and site attrition continues, and extreme amounts of time needed to download home pages (Maddux 1996). If learners' navigation skills are weak or when students do not know the particular capabilities and requirements of different search engines, it can take excessive amounts of time for learners to locate information they want or need.

It takes time and technical support to become a competent user of the Internet. In addition, many adults are computer-phobic (Starr and Milheim 1996), or are easily enticed by sites irrelevant to their learning tasks or educational goals, confronting an explosion of information not organized as in traditional libraries, and may have difficulty distinguishing more reliable and credible sites from less than reputable ones (Quinlan, 1997). Ironically, these problems can protract the time it takes students to learn in Internet-based settings. Moreover, these difficulties speak to the critical role of the instructor in designing and guiding the Internet-based learning experiences of their adult students.

INSTITUTIONAL BARRIERS AND INTERNET-BASED LEARNING

Providers desiring to increase adult education participation would do well to consider institutional barriers present in the setting or process that students must access in order to participate. Obvious institutional barriers that discourage many adults from taking advantage of educational offerings include failure to inform adults of available courses. Another is adults' unfamiliarity with institutions, their structure and the processes that must be negotiated. The less customer-service sensitive an organization is, the more institutional barriers there are that may hinder the participation of adult learners.

Internet-based-learning has the potential to remove or temper many of the above barriers. For instance, many institutions of higher education have home pages identifying them and linking users to a plethora of information about the institution. Thus, for adults who have Internet access, basic navigation skills, and the interest, the Internet has begun to solve the publicity limitations that have kept many adults from taking part in education.

As more institutions of higher education deliver or supplement delivery of educational offerings via online technologies such as the Internet, and in the process streamlining access to such courses, the Internet will serve to minimize traditional institutional barriers. Regardless of affiliation, Internet-based education providers can cut through both situational and institutional barriers through such strategies as putting online course schedules and course availability, registration capability, course catalogs, syllabi, assignments, and tutorial assistance. Instructors of large survey courses can make themselves much more available for one on one, though not face to face, contact with students in these large sections than under classic office hour arrangements.

An interesting advantage with education delivered online via the Internet is that many societal barriers sometimes encountered in educational institutions are limited if not eliminated altogether. For example, Munger (1997, p. 47) points out that as long as video is not part of Internet-based learning, interactions among participants "are usually free of race, gender, and age discrimination."

However, there are some access-related obstacles that must be surmounted if Internet-based training is to become widely available to the diverse adults needing or wanting further education. The minimum requirements of a computer, modem, and basic Internet competence or navigation skills are far from being met by all adults who need or would benefit from further education. While estimates of the number of Internet users vary (Barnard 1997, Maddux 1996), recent indicators suggest that over thirty million adults now have Internet access and that, while in the earliest days, Internet users tended to be more highly educated than average, new users are more representative of the population at large (Barnard, 1997). This trend suggests that we are beginning to solve the problem of access to the Internet. However, in the absence of educational and economic policies that would promote and support a "right to technology" (Lyman, Payne, and Ashlock, 1996), this trend may turn out to be more apparent than real.

Cluster 4: Learning Strategies

In order to take advantage of the vast opportunities afforded by the Internet for adult learners, they need appropriate strategies. Learners need information literacy involving the following abilities:

- Know when there is a need for information

- Identify information needed to address a given problem or issue

- Locate the needed information

- Evaluate the information

- Organize the information

- Use the information effectively to address the problem or issue (Brevik as cited by Rakes, 1996, p. 52)

Information literacy as defined above underscores the need for learning-to-learn, critical thinking, and problem solving skills. The need for these skills is heightened in the context of Internet-based learning. The Internet can induce information anxiety, perhaps rightly, so vast is its capacity for archiving and accessing data in many forms. In relation to such a medium (one cluster of the Model of Situated Learning), we are reminded of the need for new configurations of skills and an emphasis on the critical thinking required especially when negotiating various forms of unfettered information.

For effective Internet-based learning, adults need skills that may not have been taught or emphasized in their prior educational experiences. Adult learners need skills and strategies in navigation, creating and maintaining databases, spreadsheet use, and presentation skills (Metcalf and Nolan 1997). Educators have far to go in assisting students in developing such skills. Though the Internet is vast, its newness as a medium and ever developing nature produce constant new challenges in the area of learning skills and strategy development.

Search engines are a good example. Novices and even expert users of the Internet are hard pressed to understand the relative advantages and disadvantages of different search engines and their appropriateness for different purposes. Even as one may gain, often through personal trial and error, familiarity with a few favorites, new engines become available whose specific search capabilities are unknown. In addition, even if one has mastered the features of search engines and has a fix on the topic or question that forms the basis for a search, the very nature of the Internet as a hyperlinked web of information calls for skills, that while heretofore not as critical, are indispensable in the context of the learning medium of the Internet.

Navigating hyperlinked information calls for the highest possible familiarity with the topic (obviously a challenge for novices to a subject) to be able effectively to target needed information. Another important navigational skill is the ability to resist delving into intriguing links containing seductive information, that is, information which however interesting in its own right, is not relevant for the purpose in hand. However, a learner must at the same time be able to recognize when new found information necessitates modifying one's original goals, thus changing the nature of the search. As this description suggests, navigation skills and strategies are complex, recursive processes. Nevertheless, students will have to sharpen their navigation skills lest the Internet, its vastness, and its web-like rather than linear organization overwhelm them.

Even if a learner can successfully navigate the Internet while investigating a topic, as the student locates relevant information the question of information management comes to the forefront. Thus the need for students to develop the database, spreadsheet, and presentation skills to which Metcalf and Nolan (1997) have called to our attention. Better information management skills are needed quite apart from the Internet because of the exponential growth of information in the postmodern era. However, Internet-based learning in particular highlights the need for information management skills for learners.

Learners need skills and strategies that will give them the power to put information gleaned from the Internet into databases organized according to their own purposes and needs. Likewise, students need spreadsheet skills that allow learner-researchers to effectively and efficiently summarize and represent information from their Internet investigations in different forms, for example, tabular and graphic displays. Finally, students need a new array of presentation skills, that is, multimedia presentation strategies that will enable them to organize and communicate their findings and understandings in ways that appeal to their audiences.

Moreover these skills should be able to be learned from integrated or integratable types of software. As they heighten their awareness of the skills needed for optimized learning in an Internet-based environment, educators and learners must keep software and hardware developers apprised of the kinds of programs needed to support active and interactive learning. Software and hardware developers need to remain attuned to these needs themselves.

The capacity to apply word-, document,- and other data-processing skills, as well as navigation, database, spreadsheet, and presentation strategies in multimedia, interactive workspaces is critical for effective Internet-based teaching and learning. As this chapter was being written, little systematic attention could be found in the literature, both on and offline, concerning development of learning skills and strategies required for, or particularly appropriate in, an Internet-based learning environment. This area begs for attention in the admittedly still relatively new area of distance learning research and practice. However, Internet-based teaching and learning projects if they are to live up to the early promise and, in some cases hype, will depend on careful attention to this factor in the Model of Situated Learning—appropriate learning skills and strategies for effective Internet-based learning. Adult learners will not be able to fully explore the question of "Internet-based learning: What's in it for the adult learner?" without appropriate and effective skills.

Summary/Conclusions

One of the greatest disservices that Internet-based learning proponents can do for the field is to fall prey to an overly narrow field of vision. A constricted view of Internet-based learning can all too easily result unless we draw on frameworks such as the Model of Situated Learning. The central advantage of using such a model is its ability to rotate our focus recursively onto all the major factors that impact the learning situations of adults: (1) characteristics of adults as learners, (2) learning goals, (3) characteristics of learning media, and (4) strategies appropriate for the learning situation. These factors separately and collectively, alone and in interaction, have implications for how we design Internet-based instruction so that it can most effectively address the needs of adults.

As we have seen, adults' life situations can result in major barriers to participation in learning, for example time, money, and the effect of prior negative educational experiences that Internet-based learning has an extremely high potential to solve by providing cost-effective, time efficient educational experiences. Adult learners' goals and the goals of employers and higher education institutions, as well as the goals of trainers and educators for adult learners, represent overlapping and extensive arrays of knowledge and skills. The lifelong learning required to develop these skills within a model of continuous human potential development begs for a medium such as the Internet. The Internet as a medium is striking in its ability to promote learning through sites that archive information in databases, support the exchanges of learning communities through listservs and collaborative project workspaces, provide formal and informal classes and tutorials on almost any academic and professional subject, offer games and simulations such as mock job interviews, and host multipurpose learning centers, themselves offering rich content and exchange in multimedia formats. However, to optimize learning and militate against dysfunctional learning experiences and episodes via the Internet, learners need new sets of skills. Knowledge of the nature of and best ways to develop such needed skills remains in its infancy. To neglect research and development of learning skills appropriate and indeed indispensable to the Internet is to undermine the potential of learning in an Internet-based environment to meet the needs of adult learners.

References

Anderson, J. R. 1995. *Cognitive Psychology and Its Implications*. (New York: W. H. Freeman).

Askov, E. N. 1994. "Technology as an Instructional Strategy for Program Transitions." Paper presented at the national conference Transitions: Building Partnerships between Literacy Volunteers and Adult Education Programs (May). (Washington, D.C.: ERIC Document Reproduction Service No. ED 372 225).

Barnard, J. 1997. The World Wide Web and Higher Education: The Promise of Virtual Universities and Online Libraries. *Educational Technology*, 37 (3), 30–35.

Brookfield, S. 1990. *The Skillful Teacher*. (San Francisco: Jossey-Bass).

Cams, A., Payne, E. M., Carns, M. R., Lyman, B., Raffeld, P., and Wooley, J. 1995. "Perceived Family Environment Variables of Adult Literacy Program Participants." *Adult Basic Education*, 5 (3), 166–78.

Carnevale, A. P., Gainer, L. J., and Meltzer, A. S. 1990. *Workplace Basics: The Essential Skills Employers Want*. (San Francisco: Jossey-Bass).

CommerceNet/Neilsen Survey. 1997. (http://www.neilsendmedia.com/)

Eurich, N. P. 1990. *The Learning Industry: Education for Adult Workers*. (Princeton, N.J.: Carnegie Foundation for the Advancement of Teaching).

Kirsch, I. S., Jungeblut, A., Jenkins, L., and Kolstad, A. 1993. *Adult Literacy in America: A First Look at the Results of the National Adult Literacy Survey*. (Washington, D.C.: U.S. Department of Education, National Center for Education Statistics. http://www. ed.gov/nces/pubs/index.htm)

Knowles, M. S. 1984. *Andragogy in Action*. (San Francisco: Jossey-Bass).

Kruse, K. 1997. "Five Levels of Internet-based Training." *Training and Development*, 51 (2), 60–61.

Lyman, B. 1996. "Issues Related to Adult Literacy Education Policy and Implications for the Delivery of Literacy Services." *The State of Reading*, 3 (l), 19–26.

Lyman, B., Payne, E. M., and Ashlock, S. 1997. "State Plan for Technology Use in Adult Education and Literacy: Report of the Texas Education Agency Special Project." *Adult Education and Literacy New Technologies*. (Austin: Texas Education Agency).

Maddux, C. D. 1996. "Search Engines: A Primer on Finding Information on the World Wide Web." *Educational Technology*, 36 (5), 33–39.

Maule, R. W. 1997. "Adult IT Programs: A Discourse on Pedagogy Strategy and the Internet." *Internet Research: Electronic Networking Applications and Policy*, 7 (2), 129–52.

Martin, R. 1997. "Adult Learning on the Internet." (http://www.public.iastate.edu/ ~rmartin/ Net-learning/1-warmup.htm)

Merriam, S. B. and Caffarella, R. S. (1991). *Learning in Adulthood.* (San Francisco: Jossey-Bass).

Metcalf, T. and Nolan, S. 1997. "Technology for Educator Development: What Is It? Why Do We Need It? What Do We Hope to Accomplish?" In L. Korhonen and A. Grimes (eds.), *Proceedings of the Fourth Annual National Distance Education Conference*, Corpus Christi, TX. (College Station, TX: Center for Distance Learning Research), pp. 129–32.

Munger, P. D. 1997. "High-tech Training Delivery Methods: When to Use Them." *Training and Development*, 51 (l), 46–47.

National Center for Education Statistics. 1995. "Forty Percent of Adults Participate in Adult Education Activities." *Statistics in Brief.* (http://www.ed.gov/nces/pubs/index.html).

Prawat, R. S. and Floden, R. E. 1994. "Philosophical Perspectives on Constructivist Views of Learning." *Educational Psychologist*, 29, 37–48.

Resnick, L. B. 1991. "Shared Cognition: Thinking as Social Practice." In L. B. Resnick, J. M. Levine, and S. D. Teasley (eds.), "Perspectives on Socially Shared Cognition." (Washington, D.C.: American Psychological Association), pp. 1–20.

Quinlan, L. A. 1997. "Creating a Classroom Kaleidoscope with the World Wide Web." *Educational Technology*, 37 (3), 15–22.

SCANS-Secretary's Commission on Achieving Necessary Skills. 1992. "Learning a Living: A Blueprint for High Performance." A SCANS Report of America 2000: Executive Summary. (Washington, DC: Department of Labor).

Shotsberger, P. G. 1996. Instructional uses of the World Wide Web: Exemplars and precautions. Educational Technology, 36 (2), 47–50.

Starr, R. M. and Milheim, W. D. (1996). "Educational Uses of the Internet: An Exploratory Survey." *Educational Technology*, 36 (5), 19–28.

Tehranian, M. 1996. "The End of University?" *The Information Society*, 12, 441–47.

Tucker, R. W. 1996. "The New University. The Last Word." *Adult Assessment Forum*, 6 (4), 19–17, 7.

U.S. Congress, Office of Technology Assessment. 1993. *Adult Literacy and New Technologies: Tools for a Lifetime.* (Washington, D.C.: U.S. Government Printing Office).

Wertsch, J. V. (1991). "A Sociocultural Approach to Socially Shared Cognition." In L. B. Resnick, J. M. Levine, and S. D Teasley (eds.).*Perspectives on Socially Shared Cognition.* (Washington, D.C.: American Psychological Association), pp. 85–100.

World Lecture Hall, University of Texas. 1998. (http://www.utexas.edu/world)

Internet-based Learning and the Virtual Classroom

Deanie French, Sandy Ransom, and Steve Bett

Historically, correspondence and extension programs have delivered instruction to those living at a distance. There was a clear separation between academic departments and the correspondence office. The term distance education is taking on new meanings as academic departments begin to offer Internet-based courses as part of their teaching responsibilities.

Issues

As Internet-based learning becomes an integral part of the academic environment, there are many issues that must be addressed. The corporate world will have many of the same issues related to the delivery of training courses. Key issues include:

- Is the lecture still the benchmark for determining educational effectiveness?
- Quality control related to establishing benchmarks.
- Acceptance rate of Internet-based learning.
- Models to guide Internet-based learning development.

- Effective development and integration of Internet-based courses inherently requires intra-institutional collaboration.

- Compensation (for educators in higher education)

- Unpredictable enrollment

- Marketing

IS THE LECTURE STILL THE BENCHMARK FOR DETERMINING EDUCATIONAL EFFECTIVENESS?

The process of learning is founded in traditional lectures. Deeply held beliefs about the superiority of lecture-based education contrast sharply with the notion that technology-based education can as beneficial as the "sage on the stage." Attitudinal changes rest on the premise that any innovations in education must be at least equal to a lecture.

According to Jerald Schutte In "Virtual Teaching in Higher Education: The New Intellectual Superhighway or Just Another Traffic Jam?" (1997):

> Now is the time to consider other benchmarks than the lecture. Tom Russell of North Carolina State University has raised an important thought to consider. He has compiled a large body of research (248 research reports, summaries, and papers) that demonstrates that there is no significant difference in student learning regardless of the media used for teaching. While it is possible that none of the studies alone prove that technology-based instruction is as effective as a lecture, the sheer number of studies that repeatedly find that there is no significant differences in learning, does seem to support the conclusions that technology-based education is equally as effective as a lecture-based education.

Not only can lecture quality learning be achieved through IBL; but it can also meet emerging needs, as adults demand a wider range of options when they understand what is technologically possible. As we saw in chapter 6, adults want more responsiveness to their needs and situations. Businesses need just-in-time (JIT) training so their employees can learn *when* it best fits their schedule. Desktop learning at home or work lets the learner have more involvement and accountability in the entire instructional process.

Studies indicating significant differences with Internet-based learning and the lecture format are starting to emerge, as educators become more skilled with the technology and more courses are offered over the Internet.

An experimental design was carried out during fall 1996 in which 33 students in a social statistics course at California State University, Northridge, were randomly divided into two groups, one taught in a traditional classroom and the other taught virtually on the World Wide Web. Text, lectures and exams were standardized between the conditions. Contrary to the proposed hypotheses, quantitative results demonstrated the virtual class scored an average of 20 percent higher than the traditional class on both examinations. Further, post-test results indicate that the virtual class had significantly higher perceived peer contact and time spent on class work, but a perception of more flexibility, understanding of the material and greater affect toward math, at semester end, than did the traditional class.

In the fall of 1997 Deanie French conducted a pilot study to examine several variables, one of which was the time needed to complete course modules. There were 51 students who completed 6 different modules. Descriptive statistics revealed that time differences were not related to any one module. A one-sample t-test was used to compute significance. Significant differences in time to complete modules were found ($p < .001$). *The time to complete a module ranged from 25 minutes to six hours.* The mean was 1 hour and 39 minutes. The mode was 1 hour and 30 minutes, while the median was 1 hour and 15 minutes. The students self-reported times to complete modules and some may have exaggerated the actual amount of time needed. The point this makes is that as educators we can no longer continue to measure the learning process by the amount of "seat time" that occurs when students attend class . . . they may or may not be listening. The virtual university described at the end of this chapter aims to teach students how to learn and, with the use of technology, to cut the time needed to acquire a traditional degree from four years to two.

Hiltz (1995) presented several outcomes related to the success of virtual learning at the 1995 International Conference on Computer Assisted Learning. These studies supported the following tested hypothesis:

1. Mastery of course material in the Virtual Classroom (VC) will be equal to or superior to that in the Traditional Classroom (TC).

2. VC students will report higher subjective satisfaction with the VC than the TC on a number of dimensions.

3. Those students who experience "group learning" in the virtual classroom are most likely to judge the outcomes of online courses to be superior to the outcomes of traditional courses.

4. High ability students will report more positive outcomes than low-ability students.

The importance of the traditional lecture as being the benchmark for teaching is increasingly being questioned. "There is no evidence that the lecture model of teaching is the most effective model for the most students," says John T. Moseley, provost at the University of Oregon. "Faculty members spend much of their time conveying information. The faculty member's time can be better used," he says, "and the technology can be used for basic teaching" (quoted in Young 1997).

QUALITY CONTROL IS CLOSELY RELATED TO ESTABLISHING BENCHMARKS

This issue can be addressed succinctly. Quality control of courses begins with the expert individual educator's or trainer's standards which then must be reviewed and accepted by academic departmental peers (or in business by management) as being of quality. Obtaining peer acceptance is usually challenging as each faculty member is an expert in an area, and new concepts and ideas usually do not evoke immediate concurrence for acceptance of a new course, especially if it replaces a traditional course.

In business, a new teaching methodology is judged by its cost-effectiveness ratio.

ACCEPTANCE RATE OF INTERNET-BASED LEARNING

For many individuals, traditional lectures will continue to be a valid and preferred option for learning. The future offers many learning options that are not only equal to a lecture but may in some aspects be superior. As long as the majority of mainstream educators continue to hold on to the belief that the lecture is the only effective vehicle for learning, many potentially important opportunities will be lost.

The Internet's big growth will be in our homes. Web TVs are now being introduced for a mass market that would not buy a personal computer. As faculty and students begin to increase their consumer use of the Internet, new teaching applications will become obvious. Web applications are ubiquitous. Television networks have Web addresses, and even cartoonists are beginning to include e-mail addresses in their work. Families who want inexpensive faster communication will turn to Internet technology.

Students discover the effectiveness of e-mail when friends are at a distant location.

There is an adage that one year of a dog's life equals seven years of a human's life. It could equally apply to the Internet—one year of Internet growth equals seven years of human growth.

MODELS TO GUIDE INTERNET-BASED LEARNING DEVELOPMENT

There are few models for integrating Internet-based learning in higher education or business at the time of this publication but the growth of models will be rapid. It is important to note that there will be a need for fewer innovators because the Internet allows immediate and rapid dissemination of information and models to a global community. Following our dog adage, we should anticipate that one year of innovation through technology may be equivalent to seven years of traditional innovation.

EFFECTIVE DEVELOPMENT OF INTERNET-BASED COURSES REQUIRES INTRA-INSTITUTIONAL COLLABORATION

Most educators and trainers will need to make a concerted effort to seek out others on their campus or corporation who have experienced Internet-based learning. Pioneers in IBL are usually more than willing to share the lessons learned.

Different individuals will find different entry paths to begin the process. At our university, educators may begin through learning skills at the Faculty Advancement Center, Media Services, or through department-sponsored training and support. As noted earlier, acceptance of a course begins with acceptance by departmental peers. For many educators it is far easier to offer their courses through the correspondence office than through their department. You should be aware of institutional barriers to the adoption of technology, and make alliances with those with the experience or power to help.

COMPENSATION FOR FACULTY

Who pays for innovation? As with most educational innovation, pioneers pay the highest price as they do what they have always done—design and test learning through their own motivation and energy. We have reached a place in time where pioneers are increasingly raising questions about fair compensation. Guidelines for Internet-based learning compensation for university educators are being reviewed. Individuals are either constrained or supported by the environment in which they reside.

There is no one formula which fits all. One of the biggest concerns is whether Internet-based courses should be taught as an in-load assignment. An *in-load* assignment represents the total number of courses that an educator is expected to teach as part of his or her academic contract. *Out-of-load* teaching implies that the teacher is earning additional compensation or is teaching the course for the love of it. Another consideration would be out-of-load but with additional department compensation, especially if the course is taught concurrently with a campus-based course.

Some faculty have begun virtual teaching by contracting for courses through their correspondence or distance education components of their university. Should some of these courses now be moved from the realm of distance education offices to department offices? Distance education programs typically allow continuous enrollment and longer than one semester to complete a course. A faculty member who wishes to teach a concurrent Internet-based course with a campus-based course would have to conform to campus-based semester standards.

UNPREDICTABLE ENROLLMENT

Courses offered over the Internet can potentially enroll students from anywhere in the world. The sheer number of possible students can make even the pioneering educator tread lightly. Pilot testing of the first Southwest Texas Internet-based course was limited to two students. At that time our greatest fear was getting more students than we could handle. The first two pilot students enrolled from within our own department. One student made face-to-face contact with the faculty, the other did not. Independent evaluations from the Correspondence Office indicate that the course was highly effective for both students. We decided to use a new textbook that focused on change readiness and developed new interaction strategies. When we put our course back online, enrollment in the course did not even cover costs of development. According to Marty Byro, the course production coordinator for the SWT Correspondence Office, low enrollment is a common problem for many universities who are launching virtual education. One of the barriers to enrollment is the fact that when courses are taught through distance education, they do not count as a semester course in the financial aid base from federal sources. The primary reason for denial of benefits is based on the fact these courses don't meet traditional time frames for a semester.

MARKETING

Now that we no longer fear an inundation of students, we have begun a more aggressive marketing campaign. Ideas that we are using include:

Highlighting the course through correspondence advertising.

Advertising the course in the literature for other campus-based department courses.

Establishing links from other sites that provide information to a target group.

Advertising in traditional as well as online journals.

Encouraging students who enjoy the class to spread the word.

Visits with peers in other areas to let them know the course is available.

Adding the course address to e-mail signatures.

Our Internet-based course continues to be a work in progress in terms of delivery and administration. We consider ourselves to be pioneers in the fullest sense of the term. We do not pretend to know all the answers, but we are getting better at asking the right questions.

Anatomy of a Virtual Class

As few educators have experienced virtual learning, visualizing the process may be difficult for many people. What is a virtual classroom? What does it look like? How is the information arranged? How do students get information? How do students get feedback?

Internet-based learning is characterized by these features:

- *Time options.* Time or place does not bind students. Individuals study according to their requirements.

- *Delivery method.* Material is presented over the Internet and students locate the information through a browser such as Netscape Navigator or Microsoft Explorer.

- *Interactivity.* Students are active learners. Information is presented in short chunks with frequent involvement of the learner.

- *Hypertext linkages.* Students are presented with information that is electronically linked to related information to expand basic ideas, learn related concepts, view document sources and stimulate additional learning.

- *Multimedia.* Integrated presentation options enhance learning through sound, music, or video. (At this time, many multimedia clips run rather slowly. However, in the near future, technology is expected to allow much faster transmission.)

- *Visual appeal.* The software for producing quality Internet-based documents is easy as developing word processing documents. Built-in desktop publishing features provide a polished look with color, graphics, animation, and photographs with relative ease.

- *Rapid communication.* E-mail, chat rooms, electronic groups, and software for collaborative workstations provide options for frequent interactions. Students come to expect electronic contact within minutes or hours.

- *Collecting data and capturing information.* Electronic systems provide hard copies of student interactions, records of participation in collaborative systems, and teacher responses to questions.

- *Ease of update.* Changes and corrections to the information are simplified.

Anatomy of an Online Course

The online course, TCA 3320 "Internet, Change and LTC," developed by French and Ransom offered at Southwest Texas State University, illustrates how a typical lecture course can become virtual.

First impressions count. Students arrive at an inviting Web site, which offers them choices for exploration. Choices might include information about the course, syllabus, overview of modules, course objectives, required text, information about the author, and so forth. Technical features flow seamlessly and frustration is minimized.

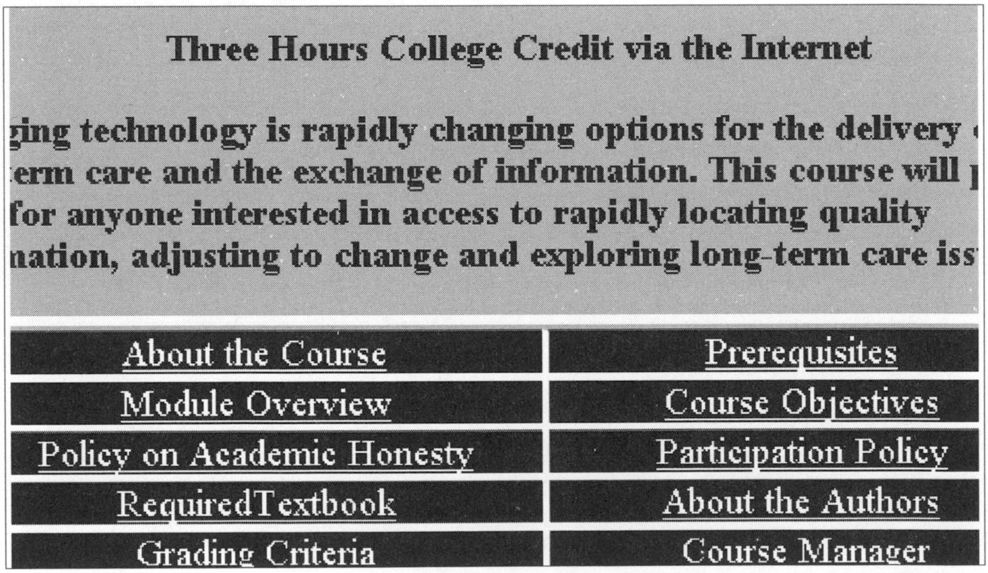

Three Hours College Credit via the Internet

ʒing technology is rapidly changing options for the delivery
ʒerm care and the exchange of information. This course will ̩
for anyone interested in access to rapidly locating quality
nation, adjusting to change and exploring long-term care iss·

About the Course	Prerequisites
Module Overview	Course Objectives
Policy on Academic Honesty	Participation Policy
RequiredTextbook	About the Authors
Grading Criteria	Course Manager

Figure 7.1 Reviewing Options

After students register, they can return to the course home page and immediately start the course by electronically pushing the button on that page. Enrollment is based on the student's schedule.

Figure 7.2 Beginning the Course

This button takes the student to a user-friendly introductory slide show. The slide show offers a link to an optional remedial Internet tutorial and ends with links to the learning modules.

The modules are password protected to provide a secure "Virtual" classroom and, by limiting access to a defined audience, may be useful in complying with conditions stipulated in a copyright permission. After students see the choices, they can select modules in

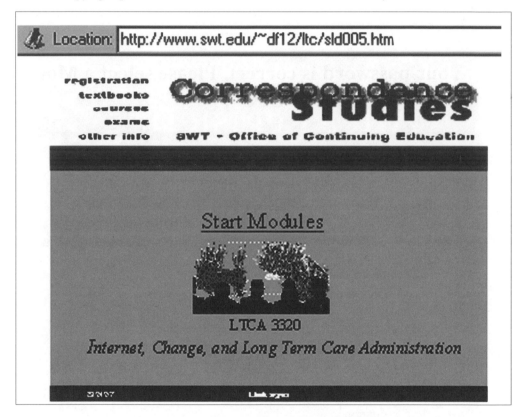

Figure 7.3 Last Slide Which Links to Modules

numerical order or create their own sequence. Some students like to quickly browse through all of the lessons to get a feel for the course—others finish them in exact order.

A completed module, "Module Five. Change and Management" is found in Appendix 7.1 at the end of this chapter. All modules begin with objectives and a discussion of the content found within the module. This virtual classroom relies on a traditional textbook as well as related Web readings. In the section, "Finishing the Assignment," the learner can see exactly what is due and when. Many of the modules have online practice tests, which help prepare for the final. All modules include an online evaluation form for the students to provide feedback regarding the components of the module and affirm its effectiveness

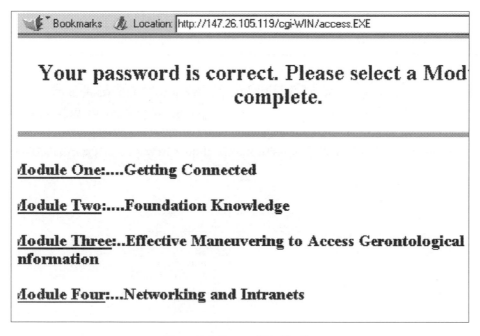

Figure 7.4 Password Verification

or identify areas for improvement. Chapter 9 covers evaluation concepts and provides examples of online evaluations.

Different Approaches to Virtual Courses

Virtual electronic education provides individual students with a higher degree of control in the learning process. Online education also requires the development and utilization of personal responsibility throughout the entire educational process. Quality online courses offered for college credit range from basic undergraduate studies to highly specialized graduate inquiry. Two examples are presented to show the diversity of approach. The first model, Learning English Skills on Line, presents the process of learning to write in ways which cannot be accomplished in a lecture format. The second model is an award winning business site for online learning.

Learning English Skills Online

English Instructor David Sharpe developed the course, English 308JW, as the first completely online, full-scale university writing course offered at Ohio University. "My hope is that the group of students will include the broadest range made possible by the Internet—students living anywhere in the world, young and old, students who are full-time or working or retired, students both inside and outside a degree program," he says. "The diversity will lead to fertile discussions and critiques in ways that a normal classroom

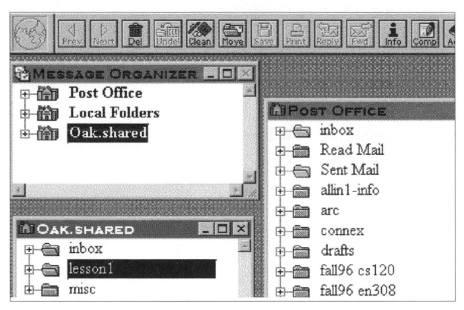

Figure 7.5 Interactive Message Organizer

can't achieve" (News release, 1996).

Figure 7.5 illustrates a screen from the collaboration software used in the course. Three windows present the main Message Organizer, the Post Office that holds all the incoming mail and personal folders, and a file called Oak Shared," which makes the folders accessible to each enrolled student.

This is a highly interactive, junior-level writing course. The instructor interweaves instructions on the development of writing skills with the expansion of the student's Internet skills.

There is a logical flow to the presentation of information, coupled with easy maneuvering among the various screens. Students interact with each other, as they are required to critique each others' assigned papers and participate in e-mail discussions and conferences. An intriguing slide show offers the prospective student a comprehensive description of the course. Up to one year is allowed for completion of the course, which includes required readings and submitted papers. Much humor is used in the instructor's presentation of course material at this excellent site.

Available online: http://cscwww.cats.ohiou.edu/~indstu/online/eng308j/

Outstanding Business Site

Dr. Jerry Siefers, has developed a site at Indiana University for the International Business Environment. Dr. Seifers won a national award for online learning presented by the University Continuing Education Association's Division of Independent Study.

This model is entertaining, captivating, and highly interactive. The use of graphics and humor take the reader beyond the normal classroom experience. This upper level courses is formatted with a mini-lecture and study questions accompanying each lesson. One year is allowed to complete nine written assignments, readings, a midterm, and a final. Each lesson focuses on one country. In addition to the business information supplied for the selected countries, interesting links specific to the country under study lead the student to more fully explore the culture of that country.

Instead of using his picture, Dr. Seifers uses an avatar, a figure representing him (see figure 7.6). This avatar also appears when a "pop" quiz is given.

Available online: http://www.extend.indiana.edu/courses/bus/busd301b/title.htm

As educators enter the virtual realm as a means of teaching/sharing material, awareness must be given to the visual format selected. Online static handouts intended for reading only mimic the traditional stand-up lecture. Students need to be interacting with the information. The use of the Internet as a teaching tool lets the instructor

Figure 7.6 Avatar Representation of the Professor

utilize color, movement, sound, conferencing and diverse linkages in the delivery of the material. From the student's perspective, one should offer a broader scope to the subject. From the professors' point of view, the Internet offers a new range of teaching possibilities.

The Virtual School Approach

Even though this chapter focuses primarily on virtual classes, the last model presented is the Malaysian approach to offering an entire degree course from a virtual school.

According to Ress (1997), "Malaysia is booming, and its capital of Kuala Lumpur—site of the world's tallest building—is the nerve center of an economic and technological transformation."

But transformation needs technology and, above all, well-educated citizens. The shortage of educated workers is a major concern for the government and the rapidly growing Malaysian private sector. In March 1996, for example, 65,000 applications were received for only 15,000 university openings, which caused near riots at some locations. And, while some Malaysians could seek to be educated overseas, this represents at an enormous expense to the country.

The Malaysian government is now seeking to build a new kind of university. Ress states that it will be "a university with no walls, but an open door to educational opportunity." Constructed around the latest information technology, it's to be a virtual school called the Universiti Tun Abdul Razak (UTAR).

UTAR is supported by Science Applications International Corp., the largest employee-owned research and engineering company in the world, under contract to Koperasi Usaha Bersatu Malaysia Berhad, one of Malaysia's largest commercial cooperatives.

Ress states that "instead of spending enormous funds and time building and acquiring the facilities to house a campus, distance education is the fundamental approach, rather than an addition to traditional educational methods."

Unlike many other distance education institutions that specialize in continuing education, UTAR focuses on the acquisition of the traditional degree (bachelor's in business and computer sciences), acquired through a mixture of live classroom broadcasts, learning on demand, prerecorded video presentations, and online software applications.

> Based and assessed on competency more than on seat-time, distance education offers the potential for more efficient delivery of services for a rapidly evolving Malaysian society. Instead of getting answers from traditional instructors, students have to learn how to find answers, and even more important, how to formulate essential questions. (Ress 1997)

The first phase started in July 1997 with students enrolled in a "pre-university" year of study, a foundation year that will prepare them for programs in business and computer sciences at UTAR. The core courses included computer literacy, intensive English, Malaysian studies, economics, mathematics and sciences.

Most courses are taught at a distance and the students are required to take workshops on independent learning skills. The first few months of study are crucial for the beginning students. With UTAR, students are given the foundation to fully benefit from all the different formats of UTAR courses, accomplishing this in half the time of traditional pre-university programs. UTAR plans to accommodate every student who passes the first-year courses.

One of the most important aspects of this type of education is that, in learning how to use the UTAR program, the students are also learning important skills in information technology to effectively function in an increasingly global society. Eventually, the program is expected to deliver most, if not all, services directly to the student's home. However, in the beginning, there will be much use of remote study centers, which will provide access to computer terminals, high-speed digital lines, videoconferencing equipment, technical support, academic advising and interaction with other students. The remote study centers provide a *place to hang out,* which is important for students who do not attend lectures or have a campus to socialize with colleagues. The learning centers also make the program more accessible to students who do not own the requisite computer, video, and telecommunications equipment necessary for the curriculum.

For expertise in producing the courses to be delivered to the students, UTAR uses help from such sources as JTG Inc., a language and educational company based in Alexandria, VA, the International University Consortium, a sixty-member worldwide organization and Virginia Polytechnic Institute in Blacksburg, Virginia. These partners provide the initial courses and training with the understanding that the Malaysian institution will develop its own courses. "Indeed, UTAR wants to have its own presence as an international provider of distance education courses. " (Ress 1997)

Virtual universities on the UTAR model appear to offer a solution to the issues of cost and access which are of equal concern in the developed world as the demand for post-secondary education and life-long learning increases. Britain's Open University and America's Western Governor's University represent a growing trend.

Summary

What is a virtual classroom? A virtual class exists on the Internet without traditional class meetings. Students retrieve information via a telephone, modem, and computer from anywhere in the world. A virtual class is unlimited by geographical location, time, or space. At the time of writing most current virtual classes are offered through already established traditional campus or business distance learning centers. Virtual classes are now beginning to enter into mainstream degree oriented academic department offerings. The general trends focus on these three factors:

1. The expanding nature of the individual role in the learning process.

2. Individual restructuring of cognitive processes and attitudinal beliefs about learning which become part of life long skills (these skills are discussed in detail in chapter 1).

3. Learning on demand will become the norm. Individual educational consumers in academia and training situations are rapidly expecting the following options:

    • Learning from home or work at their desktop without having to travel to a remote location.

- Learning at the time of day which is most convenient to the learner.

- Self-determination of time needs for studying to meet objectives.

- Global connectivity to related information.

- Immediate access to the most recent information.

- Individual access to educators.

References

"Enhancing Alberta's Adult Learning System Through Technology. 1996. (http://www.acs.ucal-gary.ca/~lidsttf/lee/pgp.html)

Hall, Nancy, 1996. "Pedagogy: Teaching on the Internet: Introduction. " August 12. (http://www.cyg.net/~jblackmo/diglib/teach-a.html).

Hiltz, Roxanne Starr. 1995. "Teaching in a Virtual Classroom. " 1995 International conference on Computer Assisted Instruction. (http://www.njit.edu/njIT/Department/CCCC/VC/Papers/Teaching.html).

Ohio University. 1996. "Independent Study Offers First All WWW Course. " November 22. (http://www.cats.ohiou.edu/~univnews/months/nov96/120.html).

Ress, Manon Anne. 1997. "Virtual University to Power Malaysia Future." *Government Technology*. (http://www.govtech.net/1996/gt/nov/nov1996-virtualuniversity/nov1996-virtualuniversity.shtm)

Russell, Tom. 1997. "The No Significant Difference Phenomenon. " January 13. (*http://tenb.mta.ca/phenom/phenom.html*)

Schutte, Jerald. 1997. "Virtual Teaching in Higher Education: The New Intellectual Superhighway or Just Another Traffic Jam?" (http://www.csun.edu/sociology/virexp.htm).

"The Impact of Technology. " 1997. September 3. (http://www.mcrel.org/connect/tech/impact.html)

University of Montana. "The University of Montana Announces Three World Wide Courses. " (http://www.umt.edu/ccesp/distance/gerontol/default.htm).

Young, Jeffery. 1997. "Rethinking the Role of the Professor in an Age of High-Tech Tools. " *The Chronicle of Higher Education*. September 28. (http://chronicle.com/colloquy/97/unbundle/background.htm).

Appendix 7.1 Module Five: Change and Management

This is an example of an online module. Underlining denotes hyperlinks to other content within the module site or elsewhere on the Web.

FOCUS: PARADIGMS, CHANGE, AND MANAGEMENT

OBJECTIVES

When you have successfully completed this module, you will be able to: (1) access Websites that clarify the concept of paradigms, (2) participate in exercises which exemplify the concept of paradigm shifting, and (3) relate concepts of paradigm shifts to change and management.

DISCUSSION

The entire healthcare industry is currently in a state of tremendous flux. Current changes and changes on the horizon will affect long term care as well as healthcare in general. Inquiry pertaining to change leads to the concept of paradigms. A *paradigm* is defined as a model or pattern, as a way of thinking about or valuing a situation, or as a framework that defines a set of rules. Paradigms can be so entrenched in day-to-day life that we are often unaware of the impact a given paradigm might have on our thinking, our actions, and our reactions. This module focuses on exploring definitions of paradigms and gaining a clear understanding of the idea of and necessity for paradigm shifts.

Of the many paradigm shifts currently affecting long term care, the policies and procedures that determine the use of restraints in nursing homes are being questioned and rewritten in facilities throughout the nation. Dr. Richard Neufeld of the Jewish Home and Hospital for the Aged in New York has conducted significant research in this area. Sites that provide more information about reducing restraint use, are

HCFA National Restraint Reduction Newsletter

The Commonwealth Fund

Journal of the American Geriatrics Society

You may have encountered the terminology "Eden Alternative" as you worked through previous lessons. The Eden Alternative, a true paradigm shift, is a nursing home management model developed by Harvard graduate, Dr. Bill Thomas. Bill and Judy Thomas, through their work in an upper New York State nursing home, identified the three "plagues" of nursing homes—loneliness, hopelessness, and boredom. The Thomases conducted research that offers antidotes to these plagues and have shared their ideals with others concerned about life quality of residents. The concept is spreading throughout the country. More information can be accessed at the following sites:

> The Eden Alternative
>
> Golden AgeNet s Eden Alternative Resources

The reading and Web assignments are interrelated from a management perspective in terms of recognizing the massive changes on the horizon in long term healthcare. The information will assist you in developing a change ready awareness as challenges are presented.

READING ASSIGNMENT

Text: Chapters 12, 14, 15, 16.

WEB ASSIGNMENT

1. Explore Elmwood Paradigms Website. Complete the graphic exercises.

2. Access the Paradigm Shift Worksheet. Construct your own Paradigm Shift Worksheet by selecting at least three paradigms that currently are operational in your personal or professional life. Determine the effects of each paradigm on current processes/performance, possible alternative paradiqms, and the potential impact on process/performance of the alternative paradigms.

3. Locate information on the Web which in some manner reflects current or anticipated paradigm shifts in the long-term healthcare field.

FINISHING THE MODULE

After you have located the information requested in part 3 of the Web Assignment

1. E-mail the URLs and/or search paths for "long term care paradigms" to Sandy Ransom.

2. E-mail Sandy Ransom the Paradigm Shift Worksheet you created, and in which you discuss your current and alternative paradigms.

3.   Consider the information regarding paradigms and relate the concept of paradigm shifting to the "Sacred Cows" discussed in Chapters 12, 14, 15. How, in your opinion, do these "cows" have relevance to long term care? Perform a "cow hunt," spotlighting sacred cows which you believe impact life quality in long term care. Identify these cows and offer any ideas you have for changes. E-mail your answers to Sandy Ransom.

PRACTICE TEST

A practice test is provided to help you prepare for the final exam. You can take it again after you receive automated feedback.

EVALUATION

You must evaluate this module using an online form. Go to the evaluation form now.
Send an e-mail message to Sandy Ransom if you have comments, questions, or concerns.

Course Manager
Revised July 30, 1997

Creating a Complete Learning Environment

Dave Harris

Using the Internet to deliver instruction takes more than creating good content, it takes a commitment to providing a complete learning environment. Providing a complete learning environment requires the creation of good content, but also requires the recognition that the content is delivered by the interface. The interface, in turn, is supported by the infrastructure. These three layers, content, interface, and infrastructure work together to provide a complete learning environment. In this chapter, we will look at the three layers, the interaction between the three layers, the instructor's responsibility for each, and the participant's responsibility for each layer.

THE THREE LAYERS

Layer	Contains
Content	Information – Exercises – Pictures – Tests
Interface	Browser – E-mail Program – Word Processor
Infrastructure	Computer – Operating System – Internet Connection

What Does it Mean to Create a Complete Learning Environment?

Creating a complete learning environment requires developing the content so a synergy is created between the content, interface, and infrastructure. This means the content allows for the limitations of the interface and infrastructure while taking advantage of features inherent in the interface and infrastructure. What is created is a learning environment that has three distinct layers, but the participant sees the three layers as one environment. The critical component here is the fact that the participant does not care if a problem lies in the interface or infrastructure. If either of those layers does not function properly, the participant will have a poor learning experience and the learning objectives will not be met.

THE LAYERS WORK IN HARMONY

It is important to go beyond creating a learning environment where the limitations of each layer is accommodated. We must strive to create an environment where the layers work in harmony. The difference in accommodation and harmony is like the difference between flying coach and flying first class. Both will get you where you are going, but the second is more enjoyable. To create harmony between the layers, we must look at how each layer interfaces with the other layers and how we can design and develop the content to create the best interaction between the layers.

INDIVIDUAL CHOICES DO NOT AFFECT INSTRUCTIONAL OBJECTIVES

As we create this environment, we must take into consideration the choices that can be made for each layer. For example, the two most common browsers today are Netscape Navigator and Microsoft Internet Explorer. If the learning environment is designed specifically for Navigator, we may find the experience using Internet Explorer to be not as rich and may actually not be as effective as we would like. Part of creating harmony between the layers is allowing for the use of different components in each layer.

EXPERIENCE IS FUN AND EXCITING, NOT FRUSTRATING AND INCONCLUSIVE

The primary goal of creating a complete learning environment is to create a situation where the instructional objectives can be met. A secondary goal is to create an environment that is fun and exciting to use. If the three layers do not work in harmony, the experience is likely to be frustrating and inconclusive. The instructional objectives may not be met, thereby not achieving the primary goal. Or, the instructional objectives may be met, but the experience may be frustrating enough to leave the proverbial sour taste in the mouth and, possibly, dissuade the instructor or participants from participating in Internet-based learning in the future.

The Three Layers

CONTENT

Content   Information – Exercises – Pictures – Tests

The content layer is the easiest to describe and the easiest to understand. The content layer is the information, exercises, tests, or other material that the instructor creates in order to create a learning situation. The content in Internet-based learning must meet the instructional objectives just like content in more traditional environments. Keep in mind that Internet-based learning is using the Internet as a delivery vehicle. However, the act of instruction does not substantially change. So, the content needs to be tailored to this delivery vehicle, but the purpose of the content does not change.

INTERFACE

Interface   Browser – E-mail Program – Word Processor

The interface layer "delivers" the content. The interface is the connection between the content and the participant or instructor. In Internet-based learning, the interface could be an e-mail program, a Web based bulletin board, a browser, a chat program, a word processor, or another program. The interface is what the instructor and participant see. It is also the layer that allows the instructor and participant to manipulate the content by selecting a path through it or actively changing it. In a more traditional environment, the interface may be face to face communication between the instructor and the participants, the distribution of handouts, or the use of reference materials from books and journals. In Internet-based learning, the interface must be married to the content in a way that the interface supports the delivery of the content.

INFRASTRUCTURE

Infrastructure   Computer – Operating System – Internet Connection

The infrastructure layer supports the interface. In Internet-based learning, the infrastructure layer includes the computer, the computer operating system, the connection to the

Internet, and the Internet services available to the instructor and participants. The infrastructure determines what the instructor and participants are able to do on the Internet, how easy an Internet connection is to make, and how fast or slow the connection will be. In a more traditional environment, the interface may be a typical classroom or training room, chairs, desks, a whiteboard or chalkboard, and the other accouterments of this style of learning. In Internet-based learning, the infrastructure should play an invisible support role. However, in today's environment, the infrastructure often makes itself known in frustrating ways and can contribute to a poor learning experience.

WHY THE THREE LAYERS WORKING TOGETHER MAKE A COMPLETE LEARNING ENVIRONMENT

Now that we have looked at what each layer contains, let us look again at how the three layers together create a complete learning environment. This time, however, let us look at how treating the three layers as a complete learning environment affects the instructional design, the participant's learning experience, and the instructor's learning experience.

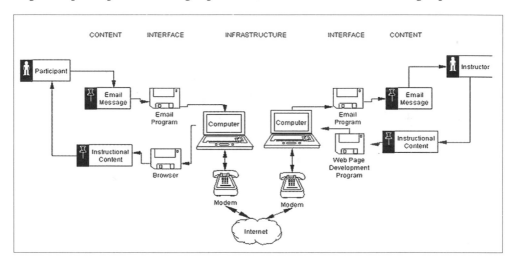

Figure 8.1

INSTRUCTIONAL DESIGN

In Internet-based learning, the Internet is the delivery vehicle for instruction. This vehicle may take a number of different forms depending on the mode of Internet-based learning that is used. A mode of Internet-based learning could be e-mail, a listserv, or bulletin board, static Web pages, interactive Web pages, chat, video conference or a combination of two or more of these. Each mode will be able to rely on a similar infrastructure. However, the interface for each mode is different. It is inherent then that the instructional design take into consideration the mode of Internet-based learning. This is necessary so that the design leverages the features of the mode and shies away from any inherent problems in the mode. For example, if the mode is e-mail, the instruction should be mainly text based and designed to be conversational between two people.

As much as possible, the instructional design should assist the participant in using the mode selected. For example, if the mode selected is interactive Web pages, the pages should contain appropriate icons and instructions so the participant can easily navigate through the content. In addition, the participant should be able to easily return to a specific location, review content already covered, submit comments or answers to test questions, and track progress.

Creating a complete learning environment requires the instructional design to take the mode of Internet-based learning into account. The instructional design must include not only the content, but must leverage the interface and the infrastructure in order to make the learning experience a satisfying one.

PARTICIPANT LEARNING EXPERIENCE

The participant may be participating in Internet-based learning to learn about the infrastructure and interface, but it is more likely that the participant is participating in order to meet the learning objectives of the instruction. If this goal is to be accomplished, the participant must see the learning experience as the totality of the content, interface, and infrastructure. In other words, the participant will be interfacing with the complete learning environment. If the participant has trouble connecting to the Internet because of an infrastructure problem and cannot quickly resolve the problem, the complete learning experience will be in jeopardy. The participant will not be saying, "The content was terrific, but the infrastructure would not work. " The participant will be saying, "I did not meet the learning objectives. This learning experience was not worthwhile. " (I'm sure you can substitute your own words for what the participant would really say.)

One of the objectives of Internet-based learning should be that at the conclusion of the instruction, the participant will want to have another Internet-based learning experience. Actually, the objective should be that the participant will look forward to having another Internet-based learning experience. This may happen if the complete learning environment works well. It will not happen if problems with the interface or infrastructure cause the participant to become frustrated or distract the participant from the learning experience.

The ultimate test of the complete learning environment is to have the interface and infrastructure recede into the background so the participant can concentrate on the rich content. This will not happen in your first Internet-based learning experiences. But, as instructors and participants gain experience in this method of learning, they will reach a point where the interface and infrastructure are familiar enough to be secondary to the content.

INSTRUCTOR EXPERIENCE

The instructor who is delivering the Internet-based learning will find the experience quite different from the traditional classroom. In the traditional classroom, the instructor and the participants are in the same proximity. The interaction that takes place is instantaneous. Feedback on comments and content are reactive. In the Internet-based learning environment, the content may be the same, but the interface and infrastructure take the place of the proximity and immediacy of the classroom.

During content development, the instructor must be aware of the complete learning environment. The content needs to be supported by and enhanced by the interface and the infrastructure. In turn, the content needs to support the interface and the infrastructure. This means assistance for participants in using the interface and infrastructure should be built into the content.

The combination of the three layers in the complete learning environment must support the completion of the learning objectives. Where the content has been matched to the learning objectives in the past, the learning objectives must now be supported by the content, the interface, and the infrastructure. The complete learning environment must support the completion of the learning objectives if the learning experience is to be successful. Since the three layers are so tightly linked that the entire system will fail if one layer fails, the learning objectives cannot be addressed by content alone.

Interaction between the instructor and participants will be carried out online in an Internet-based learning scenario. The interaction must be carefully planned and implemented. The interaction is dependent on the interface and the infrastructure. So, once again, the three layers are related in a way that cannot be separated. In order to support interaction during the learning experience, a complete learning environment must be created.

LIMITATIONS

There are limitations inherent in Internet-based learning. One of the limitations is that, except in video conferencing, face to face communication is absent. There is no opportunity to observe reactions or body language. This means messages can be misinterpreted and the opportunity for correction available in face to face communication is not available. Misinterpretations may go unresolved or may take several communications before they are resolved. In video conferencing, there is face to face contact, but it is limited. So, the same problem can arise. Another limitation of Internet-based learning is that it is a primarily reading and writing-based medium. Some content may be presented through pictures, graphics, video, or sound, but much of the content and almost all of the participant's communication will be text based. Instructors and participants who do not have good reading and writing skills will be at a distinct disadvantage.

Internet-based learning modes tend to be static modes of presentation. The content is created and posted or delivered. Once it is posted or delivered, it does not change much. Therefore, it is important to develop the content so it is rich from the beginning. In creating a complete learning environment, the content must be integrated with the interface and the infrastructure in a way that overcomes the naturally static presentation of Internet-based learning.

It is a given that, because the lack of experience and youth of the technology, Internet-based learning will have problems. Today, this is a limitation of Internet-based learning as a delivery mechanism and this limitation must be dealt with in the learning experience.

Some Examples Where the Three Layers Did Not Work Together

E-MAIL ATTACHMENTS

When working in the Internet environment, we find there are numerous programs that perform essentially the same function. Yet these programs have enough differences to cause difficulty in the learning environment. While creating a Project Management Workshop, I searched for material I could purchase to add to the workshop. I found a company in Minnesota who has a project management training program that looked interesting. Through an exchange of e-mails, the company agreed to let me preview their material. They sent me the outline and the initial chapters encoded in the message. My e-mail account is on the Microsoft Network and MSN does not currently decode some types of encoded e-mail. I went back to the Internet, searched for a free decoding program, downloaded and installed the program, then decoded and saved the file. Only then was I able to view the file. Think about how your instructional program will be affected if you are consistently exchanging encoded e-mail messages in an environment where the messages must be manually decoded.

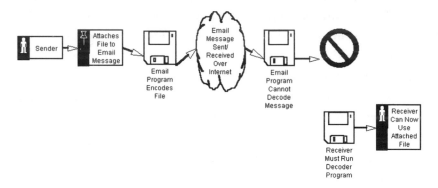

Figure 8.2 E-mail Attachment

LEARNING CONTENT, INTERFACE, AND INFRASTRUCTURE AT THE SAME TIME

QUESTIONS INTERNET-BASED LEARNERS HAVE

Content	Interface	Infrastructure
How do I find good health related sites?	How do I go back to a site I saw?	How do I connect to the Internet?
What search criteria should I use?	How do I save a site to view later?	How do I find an Internet Service Provider?
How do I evaluate a site?	How do I print the page I'm viewing?	Should I use a Mac or a PC?
Where can I find lesson plans?		

As a guest lecturer for Western Washington University, I instruct undergraduate students in a K–6 teachers program on how to access health education information on the Internet. The sessions tend to be lively and mutually informative. One of the struggles we have is learning infrastructure, interface, and content at the same time. The ultimate goal is for the students to be able to search the Internet and access information they can use in the classroom.

We start with an overview of the Internet. Then, we look at different Internet sites of interest and at Internet search tools. For the rest of the time available, the students are allowed to search and surf the Internet.

What I have observed in these sessions is that problems occur variously because of the infrastructure, the interface, and the content. However, the students who are new to the Internet do not differentiate between the three layers. For example, a student may be looking for information on a particular health education related topic. The student finds an address for a site that sounds promising. When the student tries to access the site, however, a "File Not Found" error message is received. Now, this is an infrastructure problem. The URL may have been typed wrong, the server may be down, the server may currently have too many connections, or another connectivity problem may have caused the error. The student, however, identifies the error as a content problem "I cannot find the content I want. " So, instead of an appropriate response of trying the address again, the student may inappropriately restart the search or just move on.

In another example, a student is trying to absorb the content at a site and navigate the site at the same time. Here, a problem occurs because the student is not familiar enough with the browser to understand its functionality and features. So, while trying to read the content of the site, the student is also trying to figure out how the browser works. This produces a frustrating learning experience. The student is not familiar enough with the browser to use it adequately, and cannot absorb the content of the site because of the distraction of trying to learn the browser.

Although the content, interface, and infrastructure make up the complete learning environment, learning to use each layer needs to be addressed separately and in the order of infrastructure, interface, content.

CHAT

In the academic work I am doing at Nova Southeastern University, we use chat sessions to supplement our onsite meetings, e-mail, listserv, and bulletin board communications. The chat program we use is Netscape Chat. Our experiences with the chat sessions point out the need to consider the three layers as an integrated whole, but also separate the layers to address and solve particular problems.

Before we could participate in a chat session, we had to get connected to the Internet. This is an infrastructure issue. Many of the students in our cluster had not been on the Internet before. So, they had to get their computers set up properly to make the connection.

Once our computers were set up properly, we had to download and install Netscape Chat. We then learned that Chat was no longer available. Apparently Netscape has discontinued the distribution of Chat in preparation for the distribution of Netscape Communicator.

Once the infrastructure was in place, we could begin to chat. The first one or two chat sessions were however devoted to helping each other learn the chat program and its functions. This was not by design but by necessity. The instructional objectives of the first one or two sessions were not met because of our unfamiliarity with the chat program.

When you use Netscape Chat, the messages people send come across your screen in the order they were sent. This means threads of discussion can be interwoven and difficult to follow. It took some time for us to learn how to format our messages (content) so that threads of discussion could be followed as they were displayed (interface).

Netscape Chat works with Netscape Navigator so you can show others participating in the chat a particular Web page. However, we had one or two people who were not using Netscape Chat, but were using another chat program. Their program did not have the Navigator integration feature and they had a hard time following the discussion when we referred to a Web page. This shows how the learning experience can break down when the interface (their chat program) does not match the content (the display of a specific Web page).

CHAT SERVER DOWN

What happens when the infrastructure fails? The interface and the content are not usable. Our server was down at a time when we had a scheduled chat session. With the server down, there was no easy way to let people know what was happening. We kept trying to connect, but were not successful. The session was postponed to a later date.

Making the Three Layers Work Together

Compatibility, integration, and synergy need to be considered when creating a complete learning environment. The infrastructure, interface, and content must be compatible. If the instructional design includes sending e-mail messages, the infrastructure must include an e-mail account, the interface must include an e-mail program, and the content must include the parameters for e-mail messages. Of course, the e-mail program must be one that can be used with the e-mail system in the infrastructure. And, the e-mail message parameters must be ones the e-mail program can actually accommodate.

The content, interface, and infrastructure need to be integrated so they look and act like a complete learning environment rather than looking and acting like separate pieces pasted together. If the Internet-based learning mode is static Web pages, the pages should be designed so the content looks like it belongs on the page, the pages load quickly, and navigation is natural.

If possible, synergy needs to be created between the layers. In this case, synergy means taking advantage of features in the interface and infrastructure so the whole of the complete learning environment is greater than the sum of all of the parts. For example, the content might include bookmarks to resources that are distributed to participants so they can be loaded into the chosen browser and used from the browser. The infrastructure might include installing the RealAudio player so RealAudio sound streaming can be used in the browser.

Practical Suggestions for Instructors

Having examined the three layers in a complete learning environment, we will look at practical suggestions instructors can use to create a complete learning environment.

SUGGESTIONS FOR THE CONTENT LAYER

From a learning experience point of view, the content layer is the most critical layer. Without good content, the learning objectives will not be met and the participants will have a poor learning experience.

The content, however, must be appropriate for the chosen delivery mechanism. In this case, the delivery mechanism is one of the eight modes of Internet-based learning (e-mail, listserv, bulletin board, static Web pages, interactive Web pages, chat, video conference, or a combination). In developing the content, the instructor must carefully examine three areas of instructional design: objectives, content, and evaluation.

Instructional Design

OBJECTIVES

The objectives of the instruction must be compatible with the delivery mechanism. Let us assume we are developing instruction to train participants how to complete time sheets correctly. Let us further assume we are going to use e-mail as the delivery mechanism. Our original objective may have been "Given a time sheet, correctly complete all fields on the timesheet." However, using e-mail as the delivery mechanism for the instruction makes it impossible to give the participants a time sheet as we would in a traditional classroom. So, we might want to rewrite the objective to say "At the end of the week, retrieve a time sheet from the mail room and correctly complete all fields on the timesheet."

The point here is the instructor needs to examine the instructional objectives to ensure the objectives are compatible with the delivery mechanism. Sometimes the objectives will need to be changed. Sometimes the objectives will be perfectly alright, but the way the objectives are accomplished will change. It will be rare when an instructional design can be literally ported to an Internet-based learning mode of delivery with no changes.

Once the original objectives have been examined, the instructor needs to consider whether or not new objectives are required. New objectives are required when proficiency in the interface layer or infrastructure layer are to be added to the instructional objectives. If your instruction is to use an Internet-based learning delivery mechanism, do you expect the participants to show some mastery of the interface or infrastructure during the learning experience? If the participants are to show some mastery of the e-mail program in the time sheet example above, we might add an objective that says "After completing the time sheet, enter the time sheet information into an e-mail message and send the message to the instructor." This objective is related to proficiency in the interface layer.

As a part of examining objectives for the interface and infrastructure layers, the instructor must carefully consider what skills participants are assumed to have when they begin the learning experience. If participants are expected to be competent e-mail users, this needs to be clearly stated in the syllabus. If participants are not expected to be competent e-mail users, then the instructor needs to write an objective regarding e-mail expertise and include e-mail training in the learning experience. If this is not done, then the complete learning environment model is flawed and the instructor is potentially creating a poor learning experience. The cause won't be inadequate content but the participant's inability to use the interface to access the content.

INSTRUCTIONAL CONTENT

The instructional content needs to be designed to take advantage of the Internet-based learning environment and to overcome or avoid the limitations of the Internet-based learning environment. One of the advantages of the classroom environment is instructor and participants have face to face contact. In the Internet-based learning environment, contact is limited. Great care must be taken in developing the content for the Internet-based learning environment to fully explain concepts, eliminate ambiguities, and provide clear directions for the participants. In the classroom, the instructor gets immediate feedback through body language, comments, and questions. If an explanation is not clear, the instructor can provide further explanation on the spot. In addition, the instructor's explanation in the classroom is aided by the instructor's own body language, gestures, and voice intonation. None of this exists in the Internet-based learning environment. The possible exception is video conferencing, but today's technology still does not allow the same experience as the classroom experience. In the Internet-based learning environment, a participant and instructor may need to communicate a number of times before a concept is understood, or the concept may be misinterpreted from the beginning and never be correctly understood. This situation, then, creates the requirement that more time and effort be devoted to developing the content for Internet-based learning than would be devoted to traditional classroom instruction.

The Internet-based learning environment offers several advantages over traditional classroom instruction. One of the advantages is the instruction can be delivered anywhere, anytime.

With many of the modes of Internet-based learning, the instructor and participants do not need to be present at the same time. The instruction needs to be designed to take advantage of this situation. The content needs to be self contained so a participant can use the content without the instructor's presence. In addition, the content needs to be designed with several paths. This allows the participant to continue the learning experience while waiting for a response from the instructor. If we again use the time sheet example, let us say the first field on the time sheet is the department. And let us assume the participant does not know what to put in the department field. The participant would e-mail the instructor and ask the instructor how to complete the department field. While the participant is waiting for an e-mail reply from the instructor, the participant should be able to continue with the instruction and complete other parts of the time sheet. To require the participant to stop until receiving a reply from the instructor will cause an unnecessary delay in the learning experience and most likely frustrate the participant. However, if the participant is to be able to go on to other parts of the time sheet, the content of the instruction must be developed in a way that allows continuation without completion of the department field *and* allows the participant to return to the department field when a reply is received from the instructor.

Of course, Internet-based learning provides numerous advantages that can be used to create rich content. E-mail and listservs offer the advantages of being able to track comments and responses. Web pages offer the advantages of hypertext, graphics, sound, video, and ease of distribution. Bulletin boards offer the advantage of collecting and storing all messages in one place and may offer the ability to include hypertext, graphics, sound, and video. Video conferencing offers the ability for face to face contact without having to be in the same place. These and other features are available for the instructor to use. And, the instructor should take advantage of the features of Internet-based learning. If the content is simply a port of classroom material to the Internet, the result will usually be a mediocre learning experience. Instead the content needs to be reworked to create a scenario that will enrich the participants' learning experience.

EVALUATION

Evaluation in the Internet-based learning environment must be addressed as part of the content design. This is necessary because the evaluation may be an integral part of the content itself. Let us assume for evaluation purposes, the instructor wants to track where a participant goes in an interactive Web-based learning experience. The tracking of navigation and progress needs to be built into the content that the participant sees. This is a different design than the traditional pre-test and post-test design. Internet-based learning design essentially requires ongoing evaluation. To go a step further, if we want the participant to pursue a particular direction based on the ongoing evaluation, the need to include the evaluation in the design of the content becomes even greater. For example, based on responses and navigation, it may be clear that the participant needs to go back and review some of the material; or conversely, that the participant should be allowed to skip some of the material. The evaluation and navigation that supports going back or skipping forward must be built into the content.

Interactivity

Interactivity, collaboration, small group work, large group work, and individual work are all viable scenarios in Internet-based learning. However, designing and implementing these interactivity scenarios requires the instructor to consider the content, interface, and infrastructure. The interactivity must be designed to support the learning objectives. At the same time, the interface and infrastructure that will support the content must be taken into account. Let us look at the eight modes of Internet-based learning and how interactivity can be supported in each mode.

In e-mail, the interactivity comes from sending and receiving e-mail messages. Interactivity can be developed between the instructor and all, some, or one participant. Interactivity can be developed between all, some, or two of the participants. The design of interactivity has to recognize that there is always a delay in e-mail. The delay is the time it takes for the message to be received and read by the participant or instructor. It is important to remember the time under consideration is the time received and *read*. A message may be posted to a mailbox several hours before it is actually read. In collaborative work or discussions using e-mail, it is common for messages related to a common thread to be received out of order. These limitations of e-mail must be considered in the design of Internet-based learning based on e-mail.

A listserv provides the opportunity for everyone on the list to receive all messages. In terms of interactivity, this allows several threads (or discussions) to go on at the same time. Because participants in the list generally reply to a particular message, it is easy to follow a particular thread. Listservs are, however, almost entirely text based. So, the discussions are limited to what can be conveyed in text. Participants in a list may also select the digest option. This means the participant gets all of the messages for one day in one e-mail message. Those participants are only going to get one message per day and it can take them one day to respond. The text only format and the digest option must be considered in the design of Internet-based learning based on a listserv.

Web-based bulletin boards allow the participants and instructor to post messages and reply to other posts. Generally, someone will start a discussion by posting a message. Others will reply to the original message or may reply to other replies. This creates a hierarchy of messages that, theoretically, has a logical structure. Because replies are not always posted in the appropriate place and new messages are not always created when the topic changes, the hierarchy may not be accurate. Depending on the program used, bulletin boards may be text based or may allow graphics, sound, and video. The instructor and participants have to check the bulletin board periodically to see if there are new postings. This can cause some delay in the continuation of a discussion. Designing interactivity for Internet-based learning based on a bulletin board should center on posing a problem or issue and generating a discussion around that topic.

When the instructor wants to share content with the participants that includes text, graphics, sound, or video, static Web pages can be used. However, by definition, static Web pages do not have interactivity built in. So, interactivity would need to be included using another mechanism like e-mail. A link to the other mechanism could be included on the Web pages to promote ease of use.

Interactive Web pages, on the other hand, have interactivity built in. Instead of just viewing the content, the participant interacts with the content and may interact with other participants or the instructor. Interaction could include completing a feedback form, selecting check boxes, entering search criteria, or writing sample code. Creating interactive Web pages requires some knowledge of a scripting language and some practice at creating effective interaction. This mode is probably not where the instructor new to Internet-based learning wants to start, but is probably where the instructor interested in creating a rich learning environment wants to end up.

Chat is an Internet-based learning mode that is interactive by definition. Participants in the chat interact in real time. Effective interaction using chat, however, must be planned and moderated. The instructor should pose questions or discussion topics and keep the chat on track. Otherwise, the discussion quickly breaks down into a cocktail party. One of the problems with interaction using chat is anyone can "talk" at anytime. It may be beneficial, at times, to limit who is "talking" so complete ideas can be developed. Interaction using chat requires some practice and good design to be considered a successful use of Internet-based learning.

The last mode of Internet-based learning is a combination of two or more modes. This is the most common mode as no one mode stands well by itself. However, I recommend the instructor and participants gain some experience in the individual modes before attempting to combine modes in one learning experience.

Presentation

The presentation of the content in Internet-based learning is where the content can be enhanced, become incredibly rich, or be overwhelmed by glitz and glamour. It is imperative that the instructor strike a balance between enriching the content with Internet-based learning features, the amount of effort required, and meeting the instructional objectives.

Content that is only text will be viewed as being poor instructional design even if it meets the instructional objectives. Participants in Internet-based learning expect to see and use features of the Internet environment. To not use Internet features in Internet-based learning would suggest that the wrong delivery vehicle has been chosen.

However, the features the instructor chooses to use should enhance the content. For example, graphics should add to the information being presented by the text. Graphics should not be included to spice up the text or add visual interest unless the graphics are related to and help explain the text.

There are enough features available in Internet-based learning to allow an instructor to continue to enhance the content and never finish the project. Judgment needs to be made as to how much effort should be put into creating the content for Internet-based learning.

Accommodation for Different Components in Layers

As the content is designed and developed, the instructor must also consider the other two layers, the interface, and the infrastructure. The content needs to be compatible with the interface and the infrastructure. The instructor could mandate the minimum requirements for participating in the learning experience and thereby control what can be used in the interface and infrastructure layers. Or, the instructor can decide to accommodate a range of options in the interface and infrastructure layer.

Being accommodating, however, may mean developing more than one version of the content. For example, if the majority of participants will use browsers that support frames, but the instructor also wants to accommodate participants who have browsers that do not support frames, the instructor may need to develop a frames version of the content and a no frames version of the content.

INTERFACE CONSIDERATIONS WHEN CREATING CONTENT

Remember that the content needs not only to provide the instructional information, but must also support the use of the interface and the infrastructure. When developing the content, the instructor must take into account the different interfaces and infrastructures the participants are likely to have. Let us look at two examples of how the unthinking instructor can create a problem by *not* considering the different interfaces participants may use.

DIFFERENT E-MAIL SYSTEMS

In this scenario, the instructor is developing instruction that will be delivered using e-mail. The instructor is using Microsoft Outlook for an e-mail program. Here are partial screen shots of Microsoft Outlook and the Pine e-mail program.

Notice that Microsoft Outlook has a tool bar and a printer icon on the tool bar (see the pointing finger). In the Pine e-mail program, the commands are word based.

What happens if the following instructions are included in the content: "To more easily

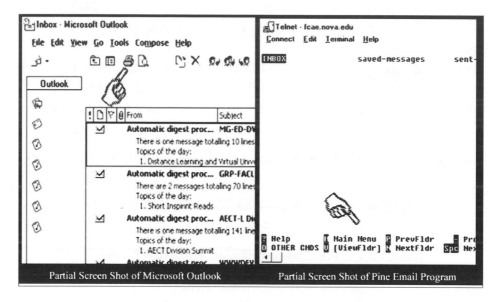

Figure 8.3 E-mail Programs Compared

read the information in this section, print this e-mail message by clicking on the Print icon in the toolbar." Participants using an e-mail program that has a Print icon will be able to follow the instructions. Participants using Pine may not readily be able to follow the instructions. The content could be changed so the instructions read: "To more easily read the information in this section, print this e-mail message." This assumes that the participants will know how to print an e-mail message. If the instructor intends to support a number of e-mail programs and provide explicit instructions, the instructor will need to include instructions for each of the supported e-mail programs.

DIFFERENT BROWSERS

This concept will be true no matter what the Internet-based learning mode is or what the interface programs are. Here are screen shots of Navigator and Internet Explorer.

Table 8.1 highlights some of the visible differences between the two browsers.

Figure 8.4 Netscape Navigator

Figure 8.5 Microsoft Internet Explorer

Table 8.1 Differences Between Betscape Navigator and Microsoft Internet Explorer

Netscape Navigator	Microsoft Internet Explorer
Uses *Bookmarks* to keep frequently accessed pages	Uses *Favorites* to keep frequently accessed pages
Change font size from the *Options menu*	Change font size using a button on the *Tool Bar*
Uses *Reload* to get the most current version of a page	Uses *Refresh* to get the most current version of a page
Calls the box where the URL appears *Location*	Calls the box where the URL appears *Address*
Has hot button links *below* the Location box	Has hot button links *to the right* of the Address box (cannot be seen in picture)

Be aware of what happens if the instructions say, "When you find a page you want to return to, save the location in your Bookmarks"?

INFRASTRUCTURE CONSIDERATIONS WHEN CREATING CONTENT

The instructor will typically have little control over the infrastructure layer. The content must be developed to accommodate the infrastructure each participant is using. The content does not have to provide explicit directions for each infrastructure imaginable. But, the content should be written with a generic infrastructure or no infrastructure in mind. If the instructor creates the content based on the infrastructure in use at the time, the content will not be valid when a different infrastructure is used. Let us look at some different components of the infrastructure layer and how differences in these components need to be considered in the content.

DIFFERENT COMPUTERS

The two most popular computers are IBM PC-compatibles and Apple Macintosh. These two computers have many similarities and many differences. A problem can be created when an instructor creates Internet-based learning content that refers to the operations of one computer. The participants who have the other type of computer must then translate the instructions. This can create a poor learning experience. The instructor should become familiar enough with the computers the participants will use to provide instructions for each type of computer. Or, the instructor should make instructions generic enough that the instructions will work with all of the computers the participants are using.

Regardless of the computer, other features of the computer can create problems for the

Internet-based learning instructor. One of those features is screen size. If the instructor creates content on a large screen using more pixels, like 1024x768, participants using a smaller screen with fewer pixels, like 640x480, may find pictures and graphics fill more than one screen. These participants will have to scroll right and left, up and down to see the whole picture or graphic. They will never be able to see the entire picture or graphic at one time. The content should be designed to accommodate either the smallest screen participants will use or the most common screen size the participants will use. If the most common screen size is used as the benchmark, some participants may have the problem described above. However, the tradeoff of additional functionality for the many in exchange for a known problem for the few may be acceptable.

Another feature of computers that can cause problems is the use of colors. If you set a number of computers side by side, display the same program or screen, and examine the colors on each screen, you will find there are variations in the colors being displayed. If your content depends on color to impart information, you should use basic colors and test your content on several computers to get a feel for the variations the participants will see. It is better to create content that does not refer to color whenever possible. For example, "Click the icon with the horse" is better than "Click the blue icon."

While we have not addressed the responsibilities of the instructor in addressing participants with special needs, he or she needs to be aware if them and the degree to which they are accomodated.

DIFFERENT OPERATING SYSTEMS

Each operating system has different features, quirks, and procedures. The content of Internet-based learning must be generic enough for the participant to be able to follow the instructions using the operating system of choice. The instructor cannot create content using a particular operating system as an example and create instructions specific to that operating system. The participants who do not use that operating system may not be able to follow the instructions and may not be able to complete the learning experience.

DIFFERENT INTERNET CONNECTIONS

When creating Internet-based learning, all of the components of the infrastructure layer must be created. If participants are using a modem to connect to the Internet, they very likely will have a 28.8k baud modem. This modem is many times slower than a direct connection over a T1 line (the typical type of connection at universities and corporations.) If the instructor creates content that has many graphics, sound, and maybe even video, the participants using the slower modem will find the Web page load time to be so slow that they may give up on the experience. The content of Internet-based learning needs to be designed to accommodate the connections participants are using.

DIFFERENT INTERNET SERVICE PROVIDERS (ISPs)

Participants connecting to the Internet through an Internet service provider (including corporate, educational, and community links) will find a wide variety of services, availability, response time, and cost. Instructors creating content for Internet-based learning should be cognizant of these differences and consider adjusting the Internet-based learning experience accordingly. For example, if a chat session is scheduled during peak Internet usage time (5 to 7pm in my area), the instructor may find some participants cannot make the session. They may not be able to connect or their connection may be so slow they cannot participate even if they can connect.

Or if participants are paying for an Internet connection by the minute, the instructor should consider designing the content so large portions can be downloaded at one time. The participants can download a large portion, work on that portion offline, and log back on to the Internet when they are ready to respond or get the next portion.

GENERAL SUPPORT CONSIDERATIONS

In providing Internet-based learning, the instructor will obviously provide support for the content. The instructor will also provide some support for the interface layer and some support for the infrastructure layer. The instructor will have to determine how much support to provide based on knowledge level and time constraints. There are three major steps to providing support in the Internet-based learning environment: (1) identify the problem, (2) separate the problem, (3) attack each layer separately.

When a participant contacts the instructor with a problem, the first step for the instructor is to determine what the problem is from the description provided. The participant will probably describe symptoms. The instructor must interpret the symptoms and reach an initial conclusion about the problem.

The next step is to separate the problem. The instructor must determine what layer or layers the problem is related to. Internet-based learning problems remain difficult. To try to address a problem that covers more than one layer makes the problem harder to solve.

The third step is to attack each layer separately. Start with any part of the problem related to the infrastructure. Fix this first. Then, move to any part of the problem related to the interface layer. Address the part of the problem related to the content last.

Content Support Considerations

There are some common problems that happen in the content layer, and some steps the instructor can take to prevent these problems. A common problem is bad or broken addresses or links. To prevent this problem, test the addresses and links. There are programs that will help you do this. For example, if you use Microsoft FrontPage to develop your Web pages, the Verify Hyperlinks option on the Tools menu will check all of the links on your pages. If the Internet-based learning experience is to last for a period of time, the links should be tested on a periodic basis.

Another common problem is providing navigation that is confusing. The participant should be able to clearly determine what content has been navigated through, what content is left, and where to go next. Providing "Next" and "Back" buttons will allow the participant to follow a prescribed path. Providing a site map will allow the participant to select a specific area to go to.

The instructor should keep in mind that the immediate feedback available in the classroom setting is not available in the Internet-based learning environment. Instructions must be written so they are not ambiguous and so they stand by themselves.

Interface Support Considerations

In considering support for the interface layer, the instructor should consider who will provide the support. Some options are:

- The instructor provides the support

- Support is provided by peers or other participants

- Support is provided by a help desk or formal support structure

- Support is not provided. It is assumed participants have a sufficient level of expertise to provide their own support.

Regardless of who provides support, the instructor should be familiar with the major programs participants will use. The instructor needs this familiarity in order to develop the content and provide support for the content layer.

The instructor should test the content with the major programs participants will use. This will catch errors in content development where the content does not match the interface.

The instructor should also have a backup plan for any Internet-based learning experience. What happens if the e-mail system goes down and messages are lost? What happens if the listserv server goes down? What happens if the participants cannot connect to the Internet to use a bulletin board? What happens if the chat server is down at the time a chat session is scheduled? These are real situations. If the instructor has not planned ahead of time for these situations, the instructor will be doing spur of the moment planning.

Practical Suggestions for Participants

The key point to remember is that Internet-based learning is relatively new. Although some distance education programs have been operating for decades, the type of Internet-based learning we are using today has only been available in the last two or three years. Any new technology will have problems. Things will go wrong. Programs will not operate exactly the way you expect them to. Consider this part of the Internet-based learning experience.

Participants can approach Internet-based learning with fear and trepidation or with excitement and a sense of adventure. I recommend the latter attitude. It will help make the entire experience more enjoyable and effective.

CONTENT CONSIDERATIONS

Participants can enhance their studies via Internet-based learning by following some simple suggestions. The first suggestion is to take notes. Take notes regarding the content, but also take notes regarding navigation, program use, infrastructure set up, and any other aspect of Internet-based learning where the notes will be beneficial later. If you go through a difficult scenario to set up your modem, take notes about the set up. Sooner or later, you will need to do it again.

Use bookmarks or favorites. This is a feature in Navigator and Internet Explorer, respectively, that lets you save the location/address (URL) for a particular Web page and easily return to that page.

Although information is available electronically in Internet-based learning, participants will still find it useful to print out some of the content. Printed copy allows the participant to make notes on the copy and to review the copy at a later time.

When writing responses, whether in real time like a chat session, or in a non-time based mode like e-mail, people tend to write what they are thinking. It is better to jot a few notes first, and then compose your message. Your messages will be more coherent and you will have a better chance of communicating your idea.

Remember that whatever you put on the Internet can easily become public. Never write anything you would not want your mother to read.

Participate fully. In Internet-based learning, the interaction between participants is just as valuable and informative as the absorption of the content and interaction with the instructor. All participants must participate fully to produce the full benefits of the Internet-based learning environment.

INTERFACE CONSIDERATIONS

The interface is the connection between the participant and the Internet-based learning experience. It is important, therefore, that the participant be familiar enough with the interface to use it effectively and efficiently. The participant should become familiar with the interface before attempting to participate in the Internet-based learning experience.

There are many programs a participant can use for each of the modes of Internet-based learning. And, new programs are released every day. (At least that's what it seems like.) Try different programs. Select the one you like. Then, *stick with it.* You do not have to stay with the same program forever, but stay with one program long enough to become effective at using the program. You will be much more satisfied learning one program and learning to use it well, than you will be if you continually change programs.

INFRASTRUCTURE CONSIDERATIONS

The infrastructure layer can be the most frustrating layer for the nontechnical participant. However, you do not need to be a technical guru to have a rich Internet-based learning experience. Learn enough about the infrastructure layer to trouble shoot common problems and get by. For the problems beyond your ability, know where you can get help. Here are some help resources:

- your instructor
- the help desk
- friends/colleagues
- books

- search the Internet

- online forums

- your Internet Service Provider

- vendors

Achieving a Complete Learning Environment

Creating a Complete Learning Environment requires the creation of a synergy between the content layer, interface layer, and infrastructure layer. This synergy between layers gets combined with the work of the instructor and the participants to create a rich Internet-based learning experience.

It is only through the combination of the three layers, the instructor, and the participants that this rich experience can be created. The content alone does not do it. The interface alone does not do it. It is the combination that creates the complete learning environment.

Web-related Assessment and Evaluation

Charles Hale and Deanie French

Link to the Past

Adding new methods for delivering instruction will not do away with one very important attendant to teaching. We must still be able to assess the outcome of any educational process. We must know whether or not the intended level of learning was achieved, whether the course or curriculum can be improved, its content needs to be expanded, or its focus needs to be sharpened. This chapter will look at the following:

1.   Evaluation terms

2.   Descriptions of online assessment tools,

3.   Design components for Internet-based evaluation, and

4.   Instruments that can be used offline or online.

Definitions and Contrasting Benchmarks: The Standards for Comparison

Educational evaluation is the collection of data relative to needs, objectives, methodology, support material, use of technology, and content to make timely decisions about instructional effectiveness. Before any evaluation can be conducted, not only should there be a common understanding of definitions; there should also be a clear understanding of the benchmarks for standards. The following table summarizes evaluation methods and criteria.

THREE CATEGORIES OF BENCHMARKS

PROCESS

Formative evaluation is the gathering of data to use in the decision-making process that occurs during a *process* such as planning, development, and implementation of a workshop, technological production, program or project.

- Addresses accuracy, design, usability, and effectiveness.
- Purpose is to improve learning rather than to grade students.
- Allows change without stopping program.
- Allows process feedback.
- Technological problems are rapidly fixed.
- New information is continually incorporated.
- Tends to be informal

Summative evaluation is the determination of the effectiveness of an event after it is completed. It is focused on *outcomes*.

- Were objectives met? What impact was there on the learners?
- What changes occurred?
- Was competence increased?
- Did benefits justify costs?
- What quantitative results can be measured?
- Was measurement normative referenced or criterion referenced or a combination?

STANDARDS

Normative-referencing compares performance of peers according to such standards as 90–100 as an "A"; 80–89 as a "B"; 70–79 as a "C" and so forth.

Criterion-referencing judges performance according to pre-set standards (based on measurable objectives) rather than performance by peers.

METHODOLOGY

Quantitative evaluation relies on numerical measures.

Qualitative evaluation takes the perspective of anthropology and makes judgements from information such as interviews, journals, group discussions, and observations.

Assessment Tools

Expressed differently, formative evaluation affects the design and construction of a training or academic course, while summative evaluation measures its effectiveness. One major advantage of Web based instruction is that formative evaluation can be more dynamic, compared to lecture-based courses.

While extremely short of quantified summative forms, the Internet abounds with examples of qualitative and formative assessment tools. These range from simple three or four question forms to forms several pages in length. The paucity of summative forms is due to the fact that outcomes (grades) are measured by objective examination. While summative forms exist, and are being increasingly used, they are not open to Internet searches, because access is restricted to those taking the course.

Completion of formative evaluation may be online or offline. Delivery of the forms may be by hand, mail, e-mail, or posting through CGI (computer term for a program that provides online feedback to participant). The method of delivery does not materially change the items to be assessed by the forms. It would seem, however, that in the case of student evaluation of a course, delivery of the form should closely follow the method used to deliver the instruction. If instruction is Web-based, but testing is done in a classroom, then have the evaluation form delivered there. If tests are conducted online, then online delivery of the assessment form seems proper. One factor that may influence the delivery method of assessment forms, however, is the complexity of designing computer-based forms. Unlike instructional pages, that are simply HTML documents, interactive forms require some background programs that are not HTML based. These programs are written in a variety of languages, and consist of an execution file, that interacts with HTML documents, but does not appear on any screen while executing. These background programs can handle online testing, grading, and recording, as well as form interpretation and data storage. You'll need to co-opt a programmer to design and implement such forms. The crucial issue, however is not the degree of technical sophistication, but that human judgment must be the final key in all assessments.

Purposes

While faculty or trainer interaction and appraisal constitute the backbone of preparing a course or training session, this is almost always done offline and by committee or by presentation and critique. In this chapter, we focus on the design of instruments to determine student reaction to the course or training session. Assessment or evaluation of any delivery of instruction, by whatever method, can be for various purposes. The most common reason for assessment is to determine the outcomes of a particular course. We may want to know what part of the instruction students retained, the overall-effect, or the degree to which they think the course will aid them in their future—a summative evaluation. We may also want to know the appeal of a course has to the student body as an elective if we are trying to build the census for a particular department or school. Sometimes evaluation is used to determine the relative merit of different instructors. Forms can also be designed in such a way as to determine the relative cost of different methods of instructional delivery. No matter how much educational institutions are dedicated to pure instruction, cost savings, consistent with the delivery of quality education, will always be an issue. Businesses, on the other hand, will consider cost as one of the prime indicators for using a particular style of employee education or training.

Before summarizing guidelines for evaluation design, we will look at several examples of evaluation forms from the Internet and critique each as to content and purpose (see figures 9.1 and 9.2).

From the University of Minnesota Digital Media Center, the following concerns a training session to promote Internet teaching usage. The session is given to:

> Supplement a two-hour workshop that allows teaching assistants at the University of Minnesota to learn how faculty and other teaching assistants use Internet tools and multimedia for teaching and learning. These World Wide Web documents will provide you with information, link you to further resources that will help in the development of your online course, and provide a space for you to communicate with others who are interested in placing their course online.

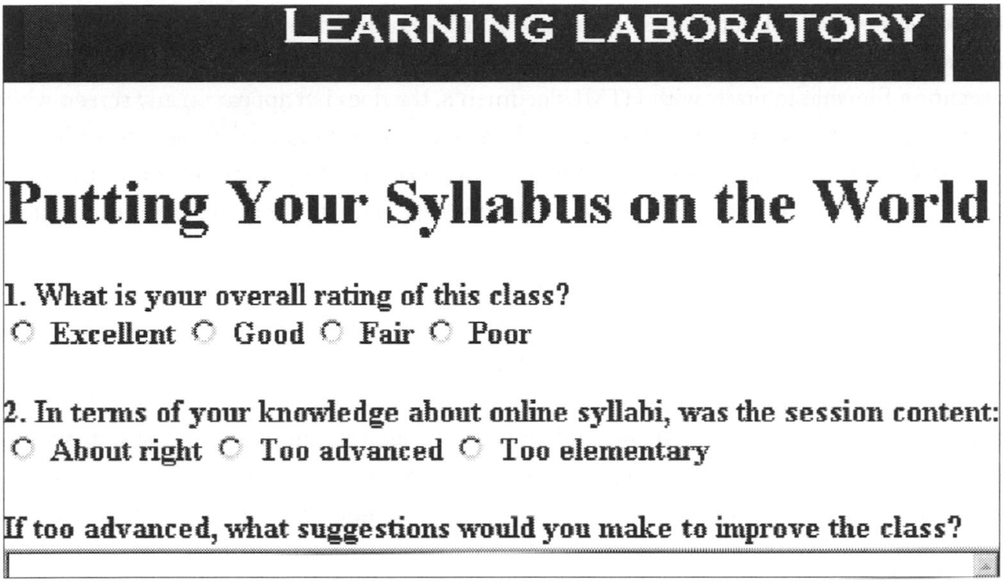

LEARNING LABORATORY

Putting Your Syllabus on the World

1. What is your overall rating of this class?
○ Excellent ○ Good ○ Fair ○ Poor

2. In terms of your knowledge about online syllabi, was the session content:
○ About right ○ Too advanced ○ Too elementary

If too advanced, what suggestions would you make to improve the class?

Figure 9.1 Putting your Syllabus on the World Wide Web; Evaluation Form

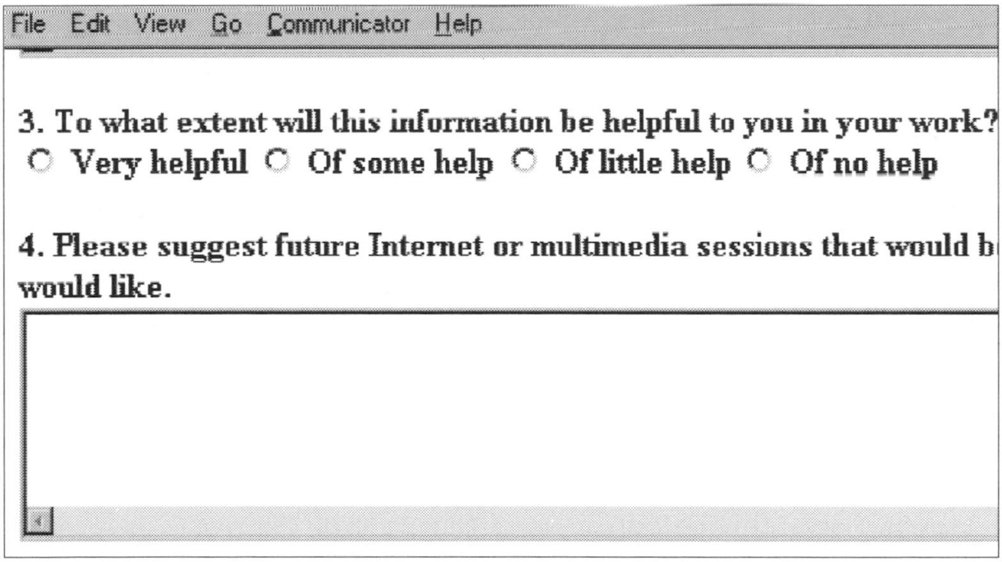

File   Edit   View   Go   Communicator   Help

3. To what extent will this information be helpful to you in your work?
○ Very helpful ○ Of some help ○ Of little help ○ Of no help

4. Please suggest future Internet or multimedia sessions that would b
would like.

Figure 9.2. Putting your Syllabus on the World Wide Web; Evaluation Form, continued

This form, placed online and with online submission, has two purposes in mind: to determine, in the opinion of work session participants, the relative value of the session and any suggestions for improvement. The form is short and to the point, and mixes check mark answers with essay type answers. The results of this evaluation will be a range of attendee opinions about the value of the training session, and in some cases, suggestions for improvement. As long as no other results are desired, the evaluation form should gain the data for which it was designed. This is a good example of the formative type of evaluation. Because the training is completed in a single session, the evaluation obtained must be devoted to future deliveries of the same or similar training functions. While it may be argued that this is a summative evaluation, because it occurs after the fact, no true measure of outcome is determined here. We do not know whether participants became more prone to use Web based instruction, or that their design skills improved. We are simply determining their opinion of the training session.

Figures 9.3 and 9.4 are used at Southwest Texas University in a correspondence course, "Internet, Change and Long Term Care. "

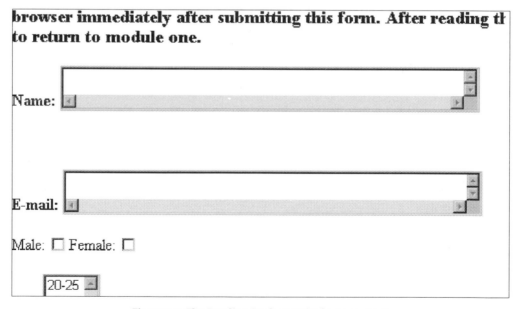

Figure 9.3 The Baseline Student Attitude Assessment

The first page of the evaluation form asks for some very basic data about the respondent. Name and e-mail address provides basic data base information. Sex and age can be used to establish baseline attitudes based on those two factors. The information can also be used to determine, over time, the "typical" student taking the course.

Behaviors related to change	Strongly Agree	Agree
I am open to new ideas.	O	O
I am anxious about change.	O	O
I feel threatened by change.	O	O
I am committed to change as an on-going process.	O	O
I anticipate change.	O	O
I will challenge the status quo.	O	O
I react to change rather than help create it.	O	O
I follow rather than lead.	O	O
I want to become more change ready.	O	O
. I expect this course to help me with change readiness.	O	O

Figure 9.4 The Baseline Attitude Assessment, continued

The second page of the form (figure 9.4) evaluates the conservativeness of the student. It also contains traps in the form of questions repeated in reversed form. The responses to 1, 4, 5, 6, 9, and 10 should mirror the responses to 2, 3, 7, and 8. Any resulting ambiguity will indicate either a student who is merely going through the motions of completing the form, or true ambiguity.

This second type of form aims to determine attitude. While more difficult to evaluate than an objective test of content, it may play a greater role in refining the course than will the content test. It can be designed so that the student receives an online response to the submission of the form. The response could look like one of the two following examples (see figures 9.5 and 9.6).

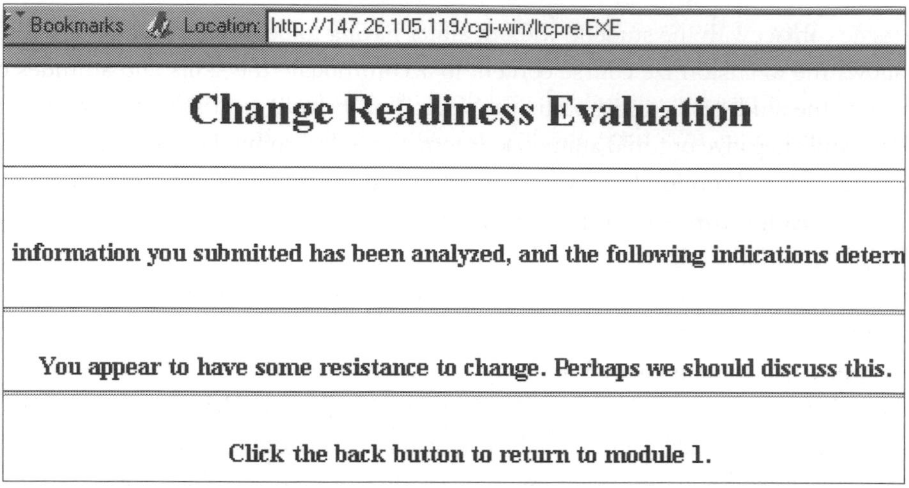

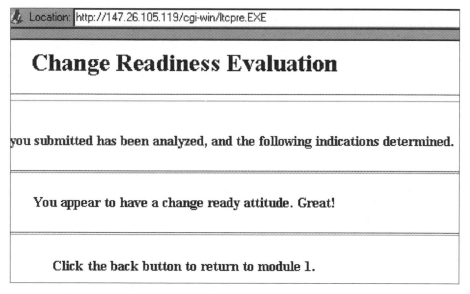

Figure 9.5 Response Returned to Students Exhibiting Negative Attitudes

Figure 9.6 Response Returned to Students Exhibiting Positive Attitudes

These responses not only let the student know that the form was submitted properly (one of the first tasks to be completed in the course), but also that I am concerned about the student's welfare. The form serves two purposes: develops a database about students and allows for an immediate contact with the student, without either having to be physically present. This form also allows me to customize course content to accommodate the skills and attitudes of the majority of the students taking a particular session of the course. If students demonstrate a predominantly negative or timid attitude to Internet-based learning, I can concentrate early on developing students' comfort levels with computers and Internet-based learning. In most cases, resistance to using a particular form of instruction results from unfamiliarity with the format, and from fear of failure in departing from preconceptions of what constitutes an acceptable learning format. When faced with a group demonstrating a negative attitude, more individual contact may be necessary to engender and nourish an acceptance of change. However, as this course is elective, students would not have signed-up without some acceptance of Internet-based learning, or at least some willingness to try new methods. If the survey shows a preponderance of positive, confident attitudes, the course may concentrate early on the more technical aspects of the subject at hand. The more information you have about students, the better you can design content to maximize the potential of student abilities and attitudes.

The next form lets students express opinions on each of the ten modules within the course. An appraisal of each module allows for greater internal fine tuning of the course than would an overall appraisal delivered at the end of the course. It also develops a database that demonstrates whether or not students' attitudes toward Internet-based instruction are changing as the course progresses. The instructor should read the form as soon as completed so that revisions can be made to succeeding modules if indicated. Modules should be immediately revised for the next session, while evaluative comments are fresh.

PLEASE CHECK THE "N" BOX FOR ANY NOT APPL

Strongly agree ...➔ *Strongly disagree*

1	2	3	4	5	N		
○	○	○	○	○	○	Q1	Objectives were clear.
○	○	○	○	○	○	Q2	Objectives were appropriate.
○	○	○	○	○	○	Q3	The textbook assignments were appropriate.
○	○	○	○	○	○	Q4	The module guidelines were effective.
○	○	○	○	○	○	Q5	Support by the faculty was effective.
○	○	○	○	○	○	Q6	The evaluation method for this module was relevant.
○	○	○	○	○	○	Q7	The evaluation method for this module was fair.
○	○	○	○	○	○	Q8	The module was beneficial in career preparation.

Figure 9.7 Module Evaluation

Figure 9.7 is another subjective evaluation form. Students are asked their opinions on the format, directions, and effectiveness of a particular module. The evaluation asks about the time required to complete the module. Data from this question permits me to determine whether content for the module under evaluation required the student to devote an appreciable amount of time for its completion, whether the content volume is appropriate for the module, or whether there is too much content and the module needs to be shortened. The remaining Likert scale questions allow for micro tuning of the module. The responses to these questions enable me to establish whether the directions for completing the module are understandable and effective, whether the content truly matches the intent of the course, and whether the available faculty support is adequate.

The last evaluation (figure 9.8) looked at is an objective evaluation, in the form of a practice test for one of the course modules. Each of the first nine modules have practice tests in the module completion section. Each is an online, interactive test, with results returned to the student immediately upon submission of the test, with wrong answers identified, and encouragement to retake the test until a 100 percent score is reached.

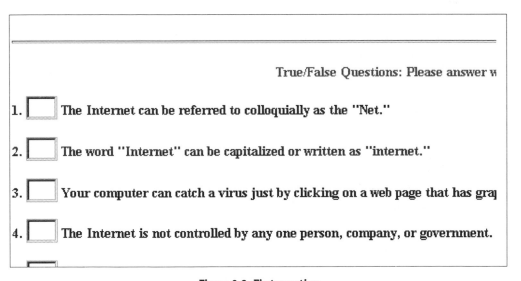

Figure 9.8 First question

The objective true/false and multiple choice questions in the practice test serve two functions. First is the classic function of determining what the student has absorbed from the module. The initial test submitted by a student for a particular module allows for determination of the extent of the student's attention to the module before taking the test the first time. A high score indicates that the student devoted sufficient time and serious study to the module. A low score is open to two interpretations; either lack of application or that she or he is the type who likes to scan the material, takes the test to determine areas of deficiency, and then concentrates time and attention to those areas. Each submission of a test for any module, by any student, is recorded in a file, and the results can be used for various purposes. Questions that are answered correctly by all students on their initial submission of the test may considered as inappropriate for inclusion in the final exam, or may need rethinking as to the exact content of the question. Questions that most students miss should be examined to determine whether they are truly covered in the module material. Questions with which students have only moderate success on the initial submission of practice tests may make good questions for the final.

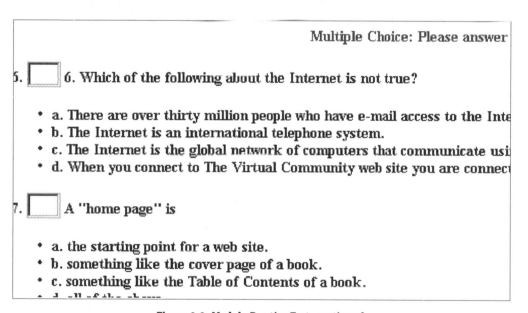

Multiple Choice: Please answer

5. ☐ 6. Which of the following about the Internet is not true?

- a. There are over thirty million people who have e-mail access to the Inte
- b. The Internet is an international telephone system.
- c. The Internet is the global network of computers that communicate usi
- d. When you connect to The Virtual Community web site you are connec

7. ☐ A "home page" is

- a. the starting point for a web site.
- b. something like the cover page of a book.
- c. something like the Table of Contents of a book.

Figure 9.9 Module Practice Test, continued

Another function of the practice test record is to discover the recovery ability of each student. If a student needs only two submissions to score 100 percent on all or most of the modules, that student is obviously being careful with restudy of the module. Students with one or two submissions are applying themselves to the module study, and this result may be used as one indicator of their final grade. Conversely, a student who needs three or more submissions to reach 100 percent, or who never submits a

100 percent test, may either not be devoting sufficient time or attention to the module, may lack necessary skills or knowledge, or may be unable to learn through this instructional technology. The practice tests and submission of required materials are used to determine 75 percent of the final grade, and careful evaluation of these is required for a fair and accurate resulting grade. Data developed over time for responses to the questions for each module can also point to ways in which the course should be fine-tuned. Some questions may need to be replaced, some retained as is, and others re-worded for effectiveness.

Learning principles serve as a guide to develop all instructional processes. The idea behind using learning theory to design and evaluate computer based instruction is to "raise questions about whether certain principles or characteristics might be easily incorporated and significantly improve the learning process" (French 1986, p. 36). The tool provided in Appendix 9.1 can be used for evaluating the use of learning principles for online learning. Key themes of evaluation based on learning principles include:

- Reducing conflict and frustration
- Repetition of concepts using variations in technique
- Positive reinforcement
- Active student participation
- Organization of knowledge
- Learning with understanding
- Cognitive feedback
- Individual differences
- Motivation

This tool can be useful in two ways: to assess current online resources such as slide shows, tutorials, and other activities already on the net; and as a guideline for formative and summative evaluation when developing materials to be used on the Web.

To reiterate, the premise behind this type of evaluation form assumes that the more learning principles used, the greater the chance of learning. Learning effectiveness, rather than perfection, is the focus.

Conclusion

Web evaluation is similar to traditional evaluation. In fact, the same forms can be used on- or offline. Online evaluation is simply a more streamlined method of reaching the same end, an understanding of the attitudes and opinions of students about a particular course. With online evaluation, recording and storage is automatic, with collation of the data and statistical analysis of the data made easier.

When you design evaluation forms, keep them simple. Do not try to accomplish too many tasks with any one form. Make sure that your audience understands the intent and questions/fields in the form. Know ahead of time how you are going to interpret the data you accumulate. Don't go fishing for any data you might pick up and then try to produce usable tuning from your catch. As you are designing, focus backward. Begin your design with clear sense of the information you need to determine. Then think about the questions to ask, and the method of answering those questions. Last, design the actual Web page to present to your evaluation audience. And always remember that as much as the aesthetics of a Web page may appeal to you, that page is merely a tool to accomplish a much more relevant result, that is, the improvement of the process of instruction and education.

Additional Resources

Gunn, Cathy. A Framework for Situated Evaluation of Learning in Computer Environments, Institute for Computer-based Learning. (Edinburgh, Scotland: Heriot-Watt University). (http://virtual.inesc.pt/rcl/rcl.45.html).

Marchio, Doug. Courseware Evaluation Database. (University of Maine). (http://kramer.ume. maine.edu/cev/eval.html).

Appendix 9.1 : Using Learning Theory to Evaluate Online Web-based Learning

This instrument was not designed to quantify the results of the Internet-based learning activity being evaluated, but rather to raise questions about whether certain principles or characteristics might be easily incorporated and significantly improve the learning process. The premise behind this type evaluation form is it's assumption that "the more learning principles used, the greater the chance of learning. "

Reducing Conflict and Frustration

1. Do links for hyperlinking documents function seamlessly?   ☐ Yes   ☐ No

2. Does the site seem inviting to use?   ☐ Yes   ☐ No

3. Are directions clear?   ☐ Yes   ☐ No

4. Does it inform the viewer how to correct a mistake if a wrong key
    is pressed when applicable?   ☐ Yes   ☐ No

5. Does the program run smoothly?   ☐ Yes   ☐ No

6. Does the web page arrangement encourage positive feeling
    toward Web use?   ☐ Yes   ☐ No

Repetition of Concepts Using Variations in Technique

7. Are key concepts covered in more than one way?   ☐ Yes   ☐ No

8. Can learners repeat portions through a menu option?   ☐ Yes   ☐ No

Positive Reinforcement

9. Do learners receive positive encouragement throughout the program?   ☐ Yes   ☐ No

10. Does the program react quickly to any response given?   ☐ Yes   ☐ No

11. Are there clues to help the learner discover correct answers?   ☐ Yes   ☐ No

Active Student Participation

12. Does the program provide exit options for the user?   ☐ Yes   ☐ No

13. Does the program allow for sufficient student interaction with the material?   ☐ Yes   ☐ No

14. Is the delay between student responses and feedback short?   ☐ Yes   ☐ No

Organization of Knowledge

15. Are lessons presented in logical sequence?   ☐ Yes   ☐ No

16.	Is there interrelationship between segments?	☐ Yes	☐ No
17.	Do they have sequence and coherence?	☐ Yes	☐ No
18.	Does the content meet specific learning objectives?	☐ Yes	☐ No
19.	Is the web an appropriate medium for this material?	☐ Yes	☐ No

Learning with Understanding

20.	Is content relevant for target population?	☐ Yes	☐ No
21.	Is the program adaptable to various levels of learning abilities?	☐ Yes	☐ No

Cognitive Feedback

22.	Are incorrect responses given feedback as to "why they were wrong" or "hints" to move them closer to a correct response?	☐ Yes	☐ No
23.	Do students have sufficient practice opportunities to learn specific information?	☐ Yes	☐ No

Individual Differences

24.	Does the menu allow sequence options?	☐ Yes	☐ No
25.	Does the menu allow choice of topics?	☐ Yes	☐ No

Motivation

26.	Does the learner get encouragement even when mistakes are made?	☐ Yes	☐ No
27.	Does the site encourage frequent interactions?	☐ Yes	☐ No
28.	Does the site personalize the information i.e. user's name incorporated into program?	☐ Yes	☐ No

(Adapted from "Using Learning Theory to Design and Evaluate Computer-assisted Instruction Software," [French 1986])

10

Perspectives on the Future of Internet-based Learning

Charles Johnson

New opportunities are presenting themselves to those of us who are preparing for the future of education. Technology is allowing us to expand our geographical reach, while at the same time supporting more efficient use of our diminishing resources. Yet, there is increasing pressure upon educators to serve an expanding market for education (Sharatt 1997). Many are rising to the occasion. The Public Broadcasting Service has recognized this trend and has seen a six-fold increase in enrolled students in the last decade. The National Technological University is serving over four hundred company sites with engineering courses borrowed from forty-five universities. The University of Phoenix's online campus offers several undergraduate and graduate programs of study. Britain's Open University enrolls distance students from all over the world.

This chapter is written for those who want to be part of this future. It is a collection of technological trends that will play a significant role in the future of Internet-based learning. We need to prepare now for these technologies as much as we train in the use of an overhead projector. These technologies are the tools of the trade for future educators. Technical issues are relegated to an appendix to this chapter in order that educators can focus on the learner first. Not all readers will be interested in the technical details.

Those educators who desire to know the future usually have to look about themselves to find the seeds of future events. Advances in Internet and computer-based technologies come fast, but are rooted in technologies available years before the advances are commonly used. In most cases, the technologies enabling major advances in Internet-based learning have been available for years, and have been only awaiting the creation of some critical, yet-to-be-developed technology to bring them to the forefront and demonstrate their utility to solving problems important to education. In some cases, the critical event may be the realization by an educator of some yet-to-be thought of application to an educational problem. The goal of this chapter, therefore, is to help educators become aware of these technologies and their potential to change our lives as teachers. We hope to not be too conservative, but rather to be bold in our forecasting. Even if wrong in our time horizon, we know it will be only a matter of a short time until the events described in this chapter are realized. The technologies discussed in this chapter are available now, and some will come into common use in little more than a year or two. This chapter will discuss how these pieces will soon come together to show us new roles as educators and learners.

Why should educators be concerned about these technological changes? After all, we will still have our usual students sitting in classrooms, learning as they have since the beginnings of modern education. Wrong! The changes to come for education are not just for the distant student. All students, near and far, traditional and nontraditional, will take advantage of the convenience and speed provided by Internet-based learning. Visualize the impact just one bold new Texas initiative will have upon higher education. The Texas Virtual College, a legislature mandated program whereby community college students will be allowed to enroll in courses from any community college listing courses in a common catalog, beginning in 1999. You may say students have been able to do this for years, transferring the credit if approved by the accepting college. The new wrinkle in this initiative is that students will be allowed to register for the course through their current community college, paying their current college, and transcripting the course as if it were taught by their current college using a course number common to all Texas community colleges. The students' current college would then be required to pay the originating college for the use of the course. All courses listed in a common college catalog for the Texas Virtual College will be available to any Texas community college student, and must be accepted by all Texas community colleges. This alone would be enough to worry many community college faculty, but an even greater concern is the rule that students can enroll in these courses even if a similar course is taught at their own community college! It will be the students' choice, and that decision could be based solely on the fact that another community college offers the course more conveniently over the Internet. Community colleges who do not make their courses available over the Internet may find themselves supporting telecommunication course development at other colleges instead of their own. The education future for Texas community colleges will arrive in 1999. Some colleges will be ready, others will not. This same educational future will arrive for Texas's four-year colleges and universities within a few years after the system is developed at the community college level, at least that is the intent of the Texas legislature. Again, some colleges and universities will be ready, while others will not.

Changes such as these have the potential to change the entire fabric of higher education, not only in Texas, but throughout the United States and across the globe. Colleges and universities may find their freshmen students enrolled in several courses taught through telecommunication, especially general education courses not related to their majors. This may lead to substantial changes in the faculty and course needs within the liberal arts, and may change the definition and governance structures of higher education. Those educators who are ready will have a much better chance to weather the storms to come. The change is inevitable. Educators preparing for these changes need to be aware of the technological foundations supporting the change. Through this knowledge, educators can anticipate change, and position themselves to prosper while serving their students. Those who do not follow the technological changes discussed below, and prepare their courses for the changes learners will demand, will be less likely to prosper in this new environment.

Integration and Overview

SELF-DIRECTED LEARNING

We have reached a point in time where both the educator and learner have become continuous learners. Boettcher and Cartwright (1997) have discussed the new "continuing professional learners—working professionals who need to retain certification, earn advanced degrees, and who need or want to update job-related skills. " Learning how to learn in this world of technology-driven education is a challenge for both educator and learner. Chapter 1 described cognitive restructuring that stresses changing the way learners think about new roles for the educator and learner as an integral part of the course. Helping learners become more self-directed in their pursuit of life-long learning skills can be a course objective in itself. Education in both the college and industrial environment is becoming increasingly presented in a self-directed format. Learners are, to use an industrial term, becoming "just-in-time" learners. Broader theoretical understanding, in many cases, is less important to the learner who needs a quick lesson on a skill required for the job at hand. Just-in-time learners need to drop into a body of knowledge to learn just the skill needed. These learners will be self-directed and ideally suited for knowledge presentation formats commonly available through the use of Internet-based learning. Internet-based learning will allow learners to access knowledge randomly through hypertext websites. For educators, this world of instant teaching will present new challenges of content organization and delivery. No longer will the educator be able to expect students to have the preferred cognitive "coat hooks" to help organize knowledge. For these learners, computer technology will provide the knowledge organization. Educators must learn how to use the organizational tools of the Internet connected computer to facilitate learning by these just-in-time learners. Learners, themselves, must learn new strategies and tools for self-directed learning. Both educators and learners have many new skills to learn as we advance into Internet-based learning.

FUTURE CHALLENGES OFFERED BY TECHNOLOGY FOR AUGMENTING LECTURES

Learning opportunities over the Internet are increasingly expanding and will become part of the routine education and training landscape. Educators will use the Internet more frequently to support or augment traditional education. The use of Internet-based course supplements can greatly expand the content options available to students. In a manner similar to how educators have used textbooks to augment their instruction, Internet-based tools will become a common course supplement. The challenges for educators will not be insurmountable. Just as educators have prepared classroom handouts over the years, those same supporting documents will be available over the Internet. The major difference will be in the hypertext linkages that can be built into the documents to facilitate understanding and learning. The only challenges facing educators are to learn how to incorporate the hypertext links into their documents and how to set up a website to support their courses. Of course, traditional correspondence programs will continue to play a key role in academic learning.

FUTURE CHALLENGES OFFERED BY TECHNOLOGY FOR VIRTUAL CLASSROOM LEARNING

Virtual classroom learning (or virtual learning) is learning that takes place over the Internet without face-to-face contact between the educator and learner. Learners use self-directed techniques to learn new knowledge at their own rate, and at convenient times and places. These goals have been served historically by correspondence and extension courses delivered at a distance. For universities, there has typically been a clear separation between the on-campus academic department and the correspondence office. This will be one of the challenges facing educators as this form of distance education becomes a routine part of the academic department. Internet-based courses will become a part of the regular workload of the college educator.

Internet learning will take many forms, from environments where only text and supporting graphics are transmitted between educator and learner, to situations where live two-way, real-time text or video interaction can take place between the educator and learner or between learners. Questions and answers must freely flow between all participants. Imagine the excitement of a totally interactive virtual classroom, where questions and answers flow freely, yet the students have immediate access to Internet-based reference material to support their arguments. In this environment, the educator must be prepared for challenges from students, and will become more of a discussion facilitator rather than an unquestioned authority. Educators will need new skills in leading discussions, as well as skills in the enabling technology. Some educators may not adapt to this new environment easily.

FUTURE CHALLENGES OF STUDENT EVALUATION

How to measure student progress will always be a challenge to educators. Internet-based learning will not be any different. Knowing who is at the other end of the Internet cable taking a test will not be easily solved. Many educators will always demand a secure proctored environment. An interesting mixture of options will be tried, including local librarians, public school officials, or other education authority figures, compensated and uncompensated. Brave educators will advance into the uncharted waters of Internet-based student evaluation. Questions could be asked which are unrelated to the content of the test, but which could help determine the identity of the student. In the middle of a test, learners could be asked for information about their family history that would not be known by anyone other than the legitimate student. This response could be compared to previously submitted student background information. Of course, there is little to prevent learners from sitting next to a person who is taking the test for them. Ultimately, with live video-conference capability, a visual examination of the test taker will be possible.

Advantages of online evaluation include immediate test score feedback to the learner and immediate statistical evaluation of objective test question quality. More in depth evaluation of written narrative responses may always require the critical eye of an educator. Internet-based learning need not preclude this more traditional form of learner evaluation.

Characteristics of the Learner

Before looking at the technologies themselves, we should examine the users or customers for these future learning opportunities. We see two types of learners needing consideration—those who are educated and somewhat affluent, and those who are less educated and looking for a way to improve income levels. There will be a market, although different, for products designed to serve both groups of customers. The more educated and affluent customers will be literate in technology, motivated to seek further education for employment and career advancement, and short on available time for education. The less educated and affluent will also be short on time, but less likely to have ready access to technology in the home. Both groups of customers will use Internet-based learning for individual needs, often as isolated learners. The less affluent, however, will not have easy access to the Internet and will be more likely to use technology in an institutional setting, either at libraries, local schools, or work. Convenience and level of learning will be the essential differences, with the convenience and mode of access factors driving decisions about packaging and marketing. For both groups, educators need to keep in mind that there will be large numbers of learners, and that for both groups, Internet-based learning will compete with entertainment for what little discretionary time is available. Those who offer successful Internet-based learning experiences will recognize this and enhance the entertainment value of the learning.

Goals for Internet-based Learning

The goals for Internet-based learning can be simply stated as quick, easy, and entertaining access to knowledge for learners and quick and easy production of courses for educators.

These goals are rapidly being realized. Internet-based learning is a developing science, with many issues yet to be resolved. These issues are being addressed in a timely fashion, with most resolvable in the near future. In many cases, bold educators are not waiting for all the issues to be resolved—they're helping resolve the issues with experimental courses where adaptations are made to circumvent the unresolved issues. Those educators who are preparing now for learning over Internet-based systems will be the first to capitalize on the opportunities to come.

Conclusions

Advances discussed in this chapter will increase the speed, ease, and entertainment value of Internet-based learning, and remove limitations and restrictions of the Internet. These advances will enable learners to interact in real-time with teachers, whether using text, graphic, or video; in static or interactive mode (as in videoconferencing). All the elements for advanced Internet-based learning are present today, and will be commonly available in no more than a year or two. We will have all the speed and storage we need to support anyone's dreams for Internet-based learning. Our challenge now will be to use it wisely.

Historically, progress in any area has been defined by human needs. We know the need for Internet-based learning is here today. We have the capabilities to begin meeting that need now. The question is whether we as teachers and learners can move quickly enough to capitalize upon these technological advances. Will our inertia and resistance to change slow these innovations? We need educators and administrators willing to experiment and move quickly to bring these technological advances to learners as soon as possible. Our limitations are not technological. Our limitations are in the minds of those who use or authorize the use of new technologies in education. Significant new opportunities abound for increased learning and efficiencies in education. The greatest immediate need is for models of instruction and learning using the Internet. Who will help lead the way by demonstrating the increased effectiveness and efficiency to be gained through Internet-based learning? Education will be an important use for these new technologies. Will you be one of the teachers who lead others into this new world of education, or will you wonder how the world came to change so rapidly?

References

Boettcher, J. and Cartwright, G. P. 1997a. "Designing and Supporting Courses on the Web. *Change* 29 (5): 10–14.

Boettcher, J. And Cartwright, G.P. 1997b. "Distance Learning: A Faculty FAQ. " *Syllabus* 10 (10): 14–15, 54.

Sharatt R. 1997. "Innovation in a Traditional Setting at Sheffield University. " In S. C. (ed.), *Open and Distance Learning: Case Studies from Industry and Education* (Sterling, VA: Kogan Page Unlimited), pp.122–31.

Sullivan, Thomas. 1998. Intel Shows Off 700-MHz Pentium II. *ENT*, 3, 7 (April 22): 22.

Appendix 10.1: Nature of Media for Learning

The issues to be addressed in this appendix include: (1) speed of access for learners, (2) ease and entertainment value of access for learners, and (3) ease of production issues. Speed and ease of access are not necessarily the same. Speed refers to the physical quickness of information flow; whereas, ease involves simple interfaces with computer systems as well as easy and entertaining delivery formats.

THE ISSUE OF SPEED OF ACCESS TO KNOWLEDGE

When discussing speed of Internet-based applications, we generally are concerned about bandwidth. *Bandwidth* of the Internet connection determines the amount of information that can be transmitted in a given unit of time. Most learners connecting to the Internet from home today are using modems with speed ratings between 33.6 K bits per second (bps), with the more advanced users having modems that communicate at 56 K bps. The problem is that communication rarely takes place at the fastest possible speed, because both ends must be able to communicate at the same rate. Many line-quality factors can also interfere with transmission speed. Even at the faster modem speeds of today, graphic intensive Internet applications do not have the transmission speed required. The situation is much worse where real-time video applications are part of the educational experience. The greatest technological advances to come for the Internet that will make the medium suitable for many educators is speed. Educators who intend to be among the leaders in Internet-based learning need to follow advances in technology related to the bandwidth problem. Internet-based learning can occur within current Internet bandwidth limitations, but significant growth in Internet-based learning will occur once this problem is solved.

ADVANCES IN MODEM TECHNOLOGY

Although slowed by a standards debate, we can expect the number of 56 Kbps modems to double every year for the next three to four years, reaching at least 20 million households by the year 2000, more than half of the homes equipped with personal computers. These modems, if supported by local telephone systems, will allow for increased use of graphic intensive Web sites and the beginnings of minimal videoconferencing. In addition, many alternative technologies are jockeying for position in hopes of solving our bandwidth problems. These technologies include ISDN and its cousins, ATM, and less expensive frame relay. As educators, we care little which technology wins, with the only exception being a preference for low cost. Since bandwidth limitations are among the greatest limiting factors facing Internet users today, we can expect significant advances to come along quickly as the industry moves to solve these problems. While educators may limit their use of real-time video today, they should be preparing for alternative delivery systems, which will enable faster video transmission over routine Internet connections in the near future.

CABLE TELEVISION AND THE INTERNET BANDWIDTH PROBLEM

An example of a technology being suggested to solve Internet bandwidth problems, leading to faster transmission speeds, are cable modems. The Multimedia Cable Network System (MCNS) standard was finalized in 1997. This standard provides interoperability between modems and connecting cable systems, allowing TCP/IP (transmission control protocol/Internet protocol—the technical specification for Internet information addressing and packaging) to be used over TV cable systems. The standard also specifies MPEG 2 (a digital movie compression standard) and the ITU (International Telecommunications Union) level B video standard. This market will take off in 1999 and 2000 after computer chip sets become commonly available from manufacturers. Data transmission speeds are expected to range between 10 and 30 Mbps. Compare that to 56 Kbps available in 1998 and we can expect significant improvement. Problems confronting this technological advance include the capacity of cable systems to use these new modems. In efforts to solve these problems, most cable systems are expected to rebuild their systems for two-way transmission within the same timeframe. New high bandwidth applications, such as video, which will be able to be transmitted over these cable modems, while increasing capabilities at the local level will lead to new congestions for the Internet backbones as multiple users of high bandwidth applications try to simultaneously transmit beyond their cable networks.

MORE FUTURISTIC SOLUTIONS TO THE INTERNET BANDWITH PROBLEM

A more futuristic, but still near-term, technological advance with the potential to reduce Internet congestion is *low earth orbit (LEO)* satellite networks. These technologies will enable high bandwidth education applications such as real-time video to be transmitted over greater distances. Low earth orbit satellites are preferred over geostationary satellites because of the shorter time (latency or delay time) required to transmit from point A to point B, promising fast Internet communication and high bandwidth. Teledesic, Alcatel's Skybridge, and Motorola's Celestri, along with several other companies, are planning high-speed satellite networks to serve Internet users. Teledesic has announced plans for a $9 billion investment in satellite technology.

U.S. government sources predict a market for up to five companies providing LEO services by the year 2005. With these satellite advances, we can expect significant improvements in Internet speeds within a few short years, enabling new, unthought-of educational applications for the Internet. Data transmission speeds are expected to range from 20 Mbps up to 155 Mbps. These speed advances will enable many stalled Internet education applications to realize their full potential—applications such as videoconferencing and graphic intensive Web applications important to Internet-based learning. Preliminary ideas about price are encouraging, with LEO pricing at about the same or lower than current high bandwidth land lines.

WORK-AROUND SOLUTIONS TO THE INTERNET BANDWIDTH PROBLEM

For many educational products delivered over Internet-based systems, there are easy solutions to the bandwidth problem readily available today. If the parts of the course content requiring high bandwidth can be delivered by some other means, then bandwidth ceases to be a problem. A solution to consider today for graphic intensive Internet educational applications is to deliver the graphic on a local medium instead of the Internet. A local medium could be a CD-ROM. Recordable CD-ROMs are relatively inexpensive and are dropping in price. Re-writable CD-ROMs are available now for a little more, but are not necessary for educational applications. Educators using these technologies can store both graphic and video content that can be linked through a local HTML page on the CD-ROM. This same HTML page could link Internet-based sites for text information and e-mail communication.

A more futuristic technology for our education desktops is DVD disk technology. *DVD* stands for either *Digital Versatile Disk* or *Digital Video Disk* depending on your reference. DVD technology will not only enhance the speed of access, but will contribute to the ease and entertainment value of knowledge access. DVD disks became available in 1998 and are expected to significantly raise the standard for recorded video on computers. Regular CD-ROM technology has only a 650 MB capacity, and is quickly exhausted by video. Current DVD-ROM disks have 4.7 GB of capacity, seven times the capacity of CD-ROMs. These single sided DVD disks can hold up to 133 minutes of video and audio, including Dolby Digital soundtracks in three different languages. Future versions of DVD disks will have 17 GB of storage, although the user will have to flip the disk over to play the other side. DVD's video, using MPEG-2 compression, is a significant improvement over VHS videotape standards. Growth projections for consumer DVD-ROM is expected to reach 31.3 million units by the end of the century, and 50.4 million units by the end of 2006 (becoming a standard item on almost every home PC before then).

Although DVD-ROM will be available for PCs first, other forms are expected to follow soon. DVD-recordable disks (DVD-R) are expected to be available imminently, but may not be practical for most of us since they are expected to sell for several thousand dollars. DVD-RAM (writable and erasable) should be available at about the same time and be equally expensive.

What impact can we expect DVD technology to have upon Internet-based distance education? Once we can get beyond the expense of DVD-recordable (even if we have to use service providers to manufacture the disks), we can expect to use DVD disks to help with bandwidth bottleneck problems on the Internet. High bandwidth graphics and movies can be easily distributed on DVD disks, instead of over the Internet, and then read through Web browser interfaces. The Internet, at least in its present configuration, will be best used for lower bandwidth transmissions. DVD disks can better deliver real-time movies, even after satellite and cable modems come into common use. Internet-based learning will best be achieved using a combination of Web server delivered text and low bandwidth graphics in combination with DVD technology linked through a Web browser interface to deliver the movie and graphic content.

FURTHER CONTRIBUTIONS TO THE ENTERTAINMENT VALUE
OF INTERNET-BASED LEARNING

MMX TECHNOLOGY

A recent technological advance that will enhance the entertainment value of Internet-based learning and speed the development of Internet-based learning is MMX enhanced microprocessors. MMX is commonly available on most computers sold in 1998 or later. The availability of specialized microprocessor instructions for highly parallel operations with multimedia and communication data will greatly improve the utility of Internet connected computers for learning applications. MMX technology enables 24-bit true color at high frame rates and multiple channels of high quality audio or video. Besides enhanced video and audio applications, we can expect improved speech recognition in future educational applications because of the additional processor instructions. Within just a few years, when the installed base of MMX capable computers becomes large enough, new applications will come to market which will require MMX technology for high-end multimedia and communication applications. MMX technology is expected to improve performance in multimedia applications from fifty to four hundred percent. Although some people associate MMX technology with game applications and discount its usefulness, MMX technology will be a significant enhancement for Internet-based learning.

PROCESSOR SPEED IMPROVEMENT AND FUTURE 64 BIT TECHNOLOGY

Processor speed enhancements to come in the next few years will fit perfectly into an Internet-based learning strategy. Under $1,000 desktop computers were available with 300 MHz Pentium processors in late 1998, helping fuel home and office computer purchases in the immediate future. These inexpensive, but powerful, home computers will be ideal for Internet-based learners. More expensive Intel 400 and 450 MHz Pentium II processors were available in 1990, and will be common by 2000. Of course, processor speed is not everthing today, where size of a processor cache can make all the difference in speed. New processor architecture by the beginning of 1999 will allow larger cache sizes running at the same clock speed as the processor itself. Intel has already demonstrated a 700 MHz Pentium II processor that will be available mid-1999 (Sullivan, 1998). By the year 2001, it is clear that we will be working with 1 Ghz or even faster processors. Think of what that speed will mean to video and the potential of future computers and the Internet for educational applications.

Whether microprocessor technology settles is questionable in itself. Digital Equipment Corporation (DEC now owned by Compaq Computers) has had its 64-bit Alpha technology available for several years now. Law suits between Intel and DEC over 64-bit patents resulted in a settlement where DEC dropped its suits and embraced Intel's newer 64-bit technology called Merced or Intel Architecture 64 (IA-64). This new 64-bit technology was developed jointly by Intel and Hewlett-Packard, and is not just an enhancement of previous 32-bit technology. With the advent of IA-64 and the apparent withdrawal of DEC, what is clear is that we are on the verge of a major transition in microprocessor technology. These 64-bit CPUs will significantly enhance the user ability to encode and edit educational video in real time, as well as any application using speech recognition.

HIGH DEFINITION TELEVISION

Another important technological advance will involve the new standards for high-definition television. The U.S. Federal Communications Commission has mandated that the top 10 television markets need to start digital TV broadcasts by April 1999. Digital TV must be broadcast in the top 30 markets by October 1999, reaching 53 percent of U.S. households. Conventional NTSC TV broadcasting is to be phased out by 2006. The consumer pressure to convert existing television sets to HDTV sets will be tremendous. Old TV sets will be useable after 2006 only with conversion boxes. What impact will this have upon Internet-based learning? To begin with, the wide-screen format of the 1080 by 1920 pixel HDTV standard will become common on computers. As we move toward a convergence of television and computers, the HDTV monitor will appear on most personal computers. Sun Computer Systems was one of the first to come to market with a 24 inch wide format monitor. Sony has disclosed plans to sell a HDTV digital disk system for home use that will record 12 GB per side, or over 1.2 hours of high-definition TV. Future Sony plans disclose storage improvements in the near future of an additional 50 percent. Although confusion has been introduced by Microsoft, Intel, and Compaq concerning the compatibility of HDTV and computers, compromises are expected soon to enable greater cooperation between the computer and television industries.

WEB-TV

Bill Gates is eagerly anticipating this new television technology, as seen by his recent purchase of Web-TV. Up to now, with the lower resolution of NTSC television, Web-TV has not been able to realize its full potential. Most users of Web-TV have not been satisfied with text resolution for most web sites. With HDTV in place, we can expect much higher resolution, and a quick convergence of web based Internet applications and the home television set. A new standard, HD-0, is slated to place computer data in the vertical blanking interval of older analog television signals. Extensions of this standard are being proposed for HDTV. Some observers have noted that, because of this advance, it may be less costly to get HDTV on a home computer than to buy a new HDTV set. Intel calls this technology Intercast. Computer users would only need to have a TV tuner upgrade card and television software (between $100 and $150) to receive HDTV on their home computers. Intercast is pure "push" technology, providing only one-way transmission. A soon to be released version of the Microsoft Windows operating system is expected to have several features to support the convergence of computers and television using this Intercast capability. Compaq has projected that between 20 to 40 million TV tuner equipped computers will be sold by the year 2000. "Push" technology will enable educators to "push" educational programming to subscriber computers connected anywhere on the Internet.

IP MULTICASTING

Another advancement will include IP Multicasting—the transmission of computer content to multiple recipients at the same time. This technology will be similar to "push" technology as seen in the program PointCast. Visualize the teaching of courses over cable or satellite networks at real-time speeds of over 30 frames per second (HDTV standards require 60 frames per second). Students will receive the program on their computers, either at home or at work, arriving at the learner's computer much like Pointcast distributes news items, and available for viewing at the convenience of the student. Augment these programs with either IP based videoconferencing or two-way IP phone conversations, and you have a soon to be realized future for Internet-based learning.

VIDEOCONFERENCING

Videoconferencing will become a major tool for Internet-based learning, as several of the above-discussed hardware and transmission technologies become available. Videoconferencing will allow two-way educational programs between teacher and student computer connected anywhere on the Internet. Recent standards have been developed including H.324, which allows videoconference transmissions over POTS-based systems (Plain Old Telephone). H.323 is another standard, which allows videoconference transmission over the Internet and interoperability between the Internet and POTS systems. Microsoft's Netmeeting videoconference program is expected to have over 50 million free copies distributed before its bundling with Windows-98. White Pine's Meeting Point and enhanced CU-SeeMe software has even more powerful capabilities including bidirectional multipoint transmission and multicast one-to-many capabilities. Envision the capability to push video-based lectures to hundreds of students using multicast technology over the Internet.

In addition to computer based technologies for videoconferencing, learners can expect the capability to participate in videoconferences over their home television sets through two-way video kits connecting over POTS systems and selling for around $500. These low prices will encourage many educators to experiment with videoconferencing for learning applications.

EASE OF PRODUCTION ISSUES

OPERATING SYSTEMS

Any technological discussion such as this must address computer operating system issues. It is in this area where the future is less clear. The dominance of Microsoft Windows, especially in newer versions of Windows 95 and Windows 98 is easy to see. The relatively unknown factors include Mac OS10+ from Apple and the BeOS from Be Computers. The future could change quickly if another operating system becomes competitive with Windows. Apple has the potential to change the future. We must guard against following the conventional wisdom that Apple is mortally wounded. Unknowns who could change the future include whether Apple releases the MacOS for multiple platforms and processors. A Macintosh computer with the ability to run either Mac or Windows software, and priced competitively could change the hardware mix on the Internet and user acceptance of high capability Internet machines. Both MacOS10+ and BeOS are worth watching closely. Legal contests between the U.S. Justice Department and Microsoft, and other countries and Microsoft could lead to a rapid change in expectations. Educators should keep a close watch on these developments, and let their opinions be heard.

More advanced operating systems are usually accompanied by more advanced software applications. These more advanced software packages will have Internet related features built-in. Office 98 software from Microsoft has several features to ease the production of HTML pages useful to even the advanced programmer. Apple, through their Claris subsidiary, have made CGI programming for Internet-based forms almost too easy with their File Maker Pro database program. Other software packages will be soon to follow.

MULTIPLE CPU MACHINES

Related to advanced operating systems is the issue of multiple CPU machines. Having more than one CPU to execute program instructions will drive a new wave of software advances. Imagine what it will mean to computationally intense graphic or video based software if program execution can be shared between several processors. These machines are available today, but even more powerful machines are planned for 1999 availability. By mid-1999, Intel will introduce a high-bandwidth architecture for high-end workstations.

Glossary of Terms

ATM. Asynchronous Transfer Mode. A dedicated-connection switching technology that organizes digital data into 53-byte cells or packets and transmits them over a digital medium. Individually, a cell is processed asynchronously relative to other related cells and is queued before being multiplexed over the line. This should not be confused with the Automated Teller Machine (ATM) devoted to banking functions.

Augmented Teaching. Augmented learning is based on the assumption that educators can enrich current teaching styles by augmenting classes to incorporate aspects of Internet-based learning. Augmented teaching styles affirm current educational styles, but, at the same time accept that courses can be enhanced with one or more Internet-based activities.

Bulletin board. An online host function that is devoted to one or a narrow range of subjects. Users can view postings, download desired items, and post messages or notices of their own to the board. The term has also come to be associated with some Web pages that perform the same type of service.

Cable. Consumer television signal delivery media.

Cognitive restructuring. Changing the way that one views and thinks about a situation, event, or opportunity.

Common Gateway Interface (CGI). Scripts or programs that run on a Web server to process forms and otherwise extend the capabilities of a server.

Computer conference. Computer-facilitated communication among members of a group, where all messages are exchanged and seen by all members.

Distance education. The organizational framework and process of providing learning at a distance. Distance education takes place when an educator and learner(s) are physically separated, and technology (i.e., voice, video, data, or print) is used as a bridge for communication.

Downloading. An electronic procedure for transferring or retrieving a file from a distant computer and placing it on your own. It is the opposite of uploading. Technically, you are also downloading any time you access a Web page with your browser—the difference being that you don't save the file to your own local computer.

Evaluation. The process of delineating, obtaining, and analyzing information in a timely fashion, about a particular subject, so that more effective decisions can be made.

Educational evaluation The collection of data relative to needs, objectives, methodology, support material, technological integration, and content to make timely decisions about instructional effectiveness.

Electronic Performance Support System (EPSS). A computer-based system that receives, stores, and disseminates organizational knowledge and information on demand.

E-mail. The use of an electronic network to send and receive messages.

Formative evaluation. The gathering of data to use in the decision-making process that occurs during events such as planning, development, and implementation of a workshop, technological production, program or project.

Frame relay. The transmission of data as a complete page or "frame" in one burst to reduce transmission time.

GEO. Geosynchronous earth orbit. Satellites that remain in one place relative to a geographical reference point. The same satellite handles all communications between points within a given range. See also LEO and MEO.

"Guide on the Side." A teacher who uses methods other than lectures to impart basic knowledge. Serves in the role of cheerleader, librarian, facilitator, and coach.

Homepage. The initial HTML document or "page" loaded when you access a site by its URL (see below) only, without defining a specific page to load.

Hypertext links. The Web address or URL, embedded in the body of an HTML document. These links automatically invoke the associated URL without you having to key in the address in the location command field of your browser. Just click and you go to the site.

Internet. A system of linked computer networks that facilitate data communication services. Often referred to as the "information highway."

Instructional development. The cyclical and systematic process of designing, developing, evaluating, and revising educational delivery methods.

ISDN. Integrated Services Digital Network

Java: A programming language that can make your Web page more dynamic with sound, animation or interactive features (also known as *applets*). However, this is not the only program that can add these features.

"Just-in-time" learning. The process of having educational access available at the time and location the learner wishes.

LEO. Low earth orbit satellites. These satellites make frequent passes over a given area, and communications are handled by the satellite currently overhead. See also GEO and MEO.

Metacognitive. Is an adjective derived from *metacognition,* which means knowing about knowing. Metacognition includes an awareness component, whereby a learner knows she is comprehending, remembering, or achieving learning goals. It also includes a control component, such that a learner knows what to do if comprehension, or achievement of learning goals, break down. Research shows that the higher a learner's metacognition, the more effective the learning.

MCNS. Multimedia Cable Network System. One cable network that can be used for different transmission services. The existing television cable networks could be used to carry digital Internet signals and telephone voice transmission. Co-axial or fiber cable would greatly increase bandwidth and increase access speed on the Internet.

MEO. Medium earth orbit satellites. These satellites make less frequent passes over a given area, but cover a greater geographical area, resulting in fewer satellites for the same coverage. As with LEO, transmission is handled by the satellite currently in range. See also LEO and GEO.

Multimedia. The technology, which is based on the blending of several different media such as, voice, video, graphics and other data in one presentation.

PALS. Peer Assisted Learning (PALS) is a system that relies on peers helping peers to learn which can enhance the learning process for all the individuals involved in the process.

POTS. The Plain Old Telephone System.

Object. Any item that is added to a Web page or collaborative work space or system such as a text, drawing, image, sound or software file.

Operational definition. The description of the process for delineating characteristics of a term.

"Sage on the Stage." A "wise" teacher standing in front of class to impart knowledge through traditional lectures to passive receivers.

Scaffolding. (1) Support which enables a student to achieve a goal or action that would not be possible without such support and (2) Support which facilitates the student learning to achieve the goal or action without such support in the future.

Situated learning. A model of learning which contains four mutually influencing clusters of factors. These factors are: (1) characteristics of the learner, (2) learning goals, (3) the nature of the media for learning, and (4) available learning skills and strategies.

Self-directed learning. The activity for which the learner takes the initiative and responsibility for completing the requirements of a particular course of study. The student provides the discipline for following the (usually) loose guidelines for the course.

Summative evaluation. The determination of the effectiveness of an event after it is completed.

Telephony. The telephone conferences which are held over the Internet.

Telecommunications. The process of transmitting or receiving information over a distance by any electrical or electromagnetic medium. Information may take the form of sound, video, or data.

Teleconferencing. The interactive communication among individuals at two or more sites using telecommunication. May involve audio, graphics, computer, or video communication.

URL. Uniform Resource Locators use a language to create Web addresses in a form which Web browsers can locate. An example of a URL is: http://www.swt.edu/~df12/feat1.htm

Virtual teaching. The educational process of learning over the Internet without face-to-face contact. Learners use self-directed learning principles to master content at their own rate, at convenient times and from the location they prefer.

Web browsers. The program that allows individuals to view Web pages, ie. Netscape.

Web servers. The computers that store Web pages and respond to requests from different browsers.

World Wide Web. An Internet service that allows the retrieval of plain text and multimedia documents. It provides a graphical, easy-to-navigate interface for viewing Internet-based documents. These documents and all the links between them comprise a Web of information.

Sources

Baber, Roberta and Marilyn Meyer. 1997. *Computers in Your Future.* (Indianapolis: Que).
Components of Software-Realized Scaffolding (http://www.cc.gatech.edu/gvu/edtech/SRS.html).
Definitions Interactive Technology and Distance Education
    (http://bscw.gmd.de/bscw.cgi/d2024405/Glossary.html)
Introduction to the World Wide Web (http://www.msn.com/tutorial/intro2.html)

Contributors

Steve Bett, Ph.D. received his doctorate in mass communications with an emphasis in instructional communications and distance education from Indiana University. In the early '70s he helped develop a NASA proposal to use satellites to deliver instruction to remote schools in northeast Brazil for the Brazilian Space Agency (CNAE). Dr. Bett currently works on problems of electronic data interchange (EDI) and the transmission of secure business documents in standard tagged digital form over the Internet and as a business case analyst for the ECRC (Electronic Commerce Resource Center) at Lamar University. In his spare time he writes articles for technical magazines, serves as the list manager for the World Language list, and writes the "Spelling on the Net" column for the Simplified Spelling Society Newsletter (http://www.oecrc.org).

Betty Collis is professor of Telelearning in the Faculty of Educational Science and Technology at the University of Twente in the Netherlands, and also Senior Researcher for Telematics Learning Technologies for the multi-faculty Centre for Telematics and Information Technology (CTIT) at the same university. She has been an active user of telecommunications in different ways in her teaching and professional life for many years, in her native

Canada as well as The Netherlands. Since 1994, she supports all her courses with WWW-based environments, and currently is in charge of an implementation project across her faculty in which the instructors of over thirty other courses are re-designing their ways of teaching and making use of the WWW as a major tool for this. See http://www.to.utwente.nl/user/ism/Collis/home.htm

Gerald Farr, BS, MA is the director of the Faculty Development Center at Southwest Texas State University. As director, he has led the mission to enhance teaching effectiveness and innovation. He has been the vanguard for stimulating faculty to use Internet-based technology for excellence in teaching. Mr. Farr has been an innovator as a biology teacher for over twenty-five years. He has been a campus leader for using Internet-based materials to illustrate and augment large-classroom lectures.

Deanie French, MSN. Ph.D. is a professor in the healthcare human resources in the Department of Health Services and Research at Southwest Texas State University at San Marcos. Her research has focused on self-directed learning since the 1970s. She has been a pioneer in the area of Internet-based learning. Every semester she actively uses augmented and virtual Internet-based approaches to learning. A virtual course, "Internet, Change, and Long Term Care," which was co-developed with Sandy Ransom was nominated for the 1998 award for distinguished independent study for online learning. She has numerous publications and presentations related to self-directed learning. (http://www.swt.edu/~df12/ltc/ad2.htm)

Charles Hale, BBA, MSHP, has been involved in designing and developing software for business functions for about fifteen years. During the last three years, he has expanded his attention to developing Web software, which can be used to supplement or to relieve people from the more mundane aspects of education. These efforts include designing online testing and grading programs, statistical analysis programs, and evaluation and survey applications. (http://www.ecpi.com/~chale/)

David B. Harris provides strategic planning and implementation management consulting services. He specializes in using emerging technologies to improve corporate, group, and individual performance. Mr. Harris assists his clients in the modifications of their organizational structure and business processes that must accompany any implementation of a new technology. He has experience in the banking, brokerage, communications, computer, consulting, education, insurance, manufacturing, retail, and software industries. Mr.Harris has consulted with companies around the world. He has over seventeen years experience in information technology including experienceas a consultant and educator. In addition to his consulting practice, Mr. Harris is currently pursuing a doctorate of education (Ed.D.) degree at Nova Southeastern University. His area of specialty is instructional technology and distance education (http://www.htcs.com/).

Lori Hooks, MSHP, is a 1998 graduate from Southwest Texas State University with a major in Healthcare Human Resources. In 1997, she was given the "Leaders for 2000" award for outstanding achievement, including the development of creative Web pages.

Charles Johnson, Ph.D. is the chairman, Department of Health Services and Research at Southwest Texas State University at San Marcos. He has been a consistent leader in faculty development for Internet-based teaching. Dr. Johnson began his leadership role in using microcomputers for classes, beginning as early as 1977, with some of the first available microcomputers. He has consistently chaired or served in futurist task forces and committees. Dr. Johnson has been recognized as an outstanding teacher by the School of Health Professions, as well as, by SWT University. He has written publications and presentations related to futurist thinking and telecommunications. Dr. Johnson has led master's theses in the advanced applications for Internet Web sites in the use of statistical software and video. He has a consistent record of community service in Boy Scouts and civic organizations (http://www.swt.edu/~cjo1).

Barbara G. Lyman, Ph.D., is a professor in the Department of Educational Administration and Psychological Services at Southwest Texas State University. She coordinates and teaches in the graduate program in developmental and adult education. She also serves as associate director of Human Resources. She has taught in higher education for a number of years and is grateful for the advent of Internet-based learning. When not engaged in writing, committee work, and Internet-based or face-to-face teaching and learning, she works at preserving flora and fauna around her residence in Texas Hill Country (http://bluesky.mediasrv.swt.edu/edp5363/).

Enrico Meeuwsen completed his teacher training as a physics teacher in The Netherlands and is in the final stages of completion of a subsequent degree program in the Faculty of Educational Science and Technology. During this period, he and Betty Collis worked closely together on the design and instruction of several courses making heavy use of integrated WWW-based support environments. He is now completing his graduate thesis work in Africa, designing and building a WWW-based support environment for a network of teacher-training institutions.

Sandy Ransom is currently director of the Institute for Quality Improvement in Long Term Health Care at Southwest Texas State University at San Marcos. In that capacity she has served as the principal investigator and/or coordinator of twelve research projects. She is a Certified Eden Associate and is the regional coordinator for Eden Alternative Region 7, a six-state region. She has published in national professional journals and has conducted presentations and seminars regarding innovations in nursing home care throughout Texas and the nation. She emphasizes technology as one way to enhance quality in long term care. She currently co-owns (with Deanie French), the electronic list, LTC-Q (Long Term Care Quality) (http://www.health.swt.edu/ltci/ltci.html).

Index

Index of Internet Resources

LISTSERVS

To subscribe to the Discussion Group for Training and Development **(TRDEV-L)** send email to **LISTSERV@LISTS.PSU.EDU** with the following, and only the following, in the body of the message:SUBSCRIBE TRDEV-L your name (e.g. Deanie French). p. 67

For information about TRDEV-L , the listserv for training and development, try:
train.ed.psu.edu/trdev-l/welcome.html p. 90

CHANGE listserv. This list is for anyone in industry or education who wants to explore initiating and sustaining change. To subscribe to this list, send an e-mail to **MAJORDOMO@MINDSPRING.COM.** In the text of the message, write subscribe CHANGE. p. 90

The List of Lists
www.catalog.com/vivian/interest-group-search.html p. 91

Tile.Net List
www.tile.net/tile/listserv/index.html p. 91

NEWSLETTERS

Quick Training Tips Newsletter, send an e-mail with "subscribe tips" in the subject line to **loretta@panix.com.** p. 89

SquareOne Technology Newsletter
www.squareonetech.com/newsletr.html p. 89

ON-LINE UNIVERSITIES

Hardwick Publications, Inc. offers online continuing education credit courses for CPAs. The course list and information can be accessed at
www.bestcpe.com/courses.htm. p. 95

Hart Crowser hosts the Online Institute. There is a demonstration course as well as courses that can be taken for a fee.
www.supportonline.com p. 95

ZDNet University (ZDU) also offers online courses. The courses are Internet and technology related.
www.zdu.com/. p. 95

TECHNOLOGICAL EVALUATIONS

Components of Software-Realized Scaffolding
www.cc.gatech.edu/gvu/edtech/SRS.html p. 202

Cathy Gunn, "A Framework for Situated Evaluation of Learning in Computer Environments, Institute for Computer-based Learning "
www.virtual.inesc.pt/rct/rct.45.html p. 177

Doug Marchio, "Courseware Evaluation Database"
www.kramer.ume.maine.edu/cev/eval.html p. 177

University of Maine, "Definitions for User Interface Rating Tools"
www.kramer.ume.maine.edu/cev/defs.html#cog p. 86

David Wooley, "Choosing Web Conferencing Software"
www.umuc.edu/iuc/cmc96/papers/wool-p.html p. 86

THINKING CRITICALLY, EVALUATING AND INTERACTING

Allen Communication
www.choice.net/~prosys/software.htm p. 86

Esther Grassing, "Thinking Critically about World Wide Web Resources"
www.library.ucla.edu/libraries/college/instruct/critical.htm p. 83

Cara Hickman, "Architects, Architecture and the Internet"
www.arch.unsw.edu.au/subjects/arch/resproj/hickman/netarch.htm p. 86

Tim Kindberg, "A Framework for Collaboration and Interaction Across the Internet"
www.dcs.qmw.ac.uk/research/distrib/Mushroom/CSCWWeb.html p. 86

WWW CyberGuide Ratings for Content Evaluation
www.cyberbee.com/guide1.html p. 83